Smoking and the Workplace

Smoking and the Workplace

ISSUES AND ANSWERS FOR HUMAN RESOURCES PROFESSIONALS

William M. Timmins

and

Clark Brighton Timmins

Foreword by U.S. SENATOR ORRIN G. HATCH

Q

QUORUM BOOKS

New York • Westport, Connecticut • London

Library of Congress Cataloging-in-Publication Data

Timmins, William M.
  Smoking and the workplace : issues and answers for human resources
professionals / William M. Timmins and Clark Brighton Timmins ;
foreword by Orrin Hatch.
      p.   cm.
  Bibliography: p.
  Includes index.
  ISBN 0-89930-423-0 (lib. bdg. : alk. paper)
  1. Smoking in the workplace—United States.   I. Timmins, Clark
Brighton.   II. Title.
HF5549.5.S55T56   1989
658.3′82—dc19   88-39742

British Library Cataloguing in Publication Data is available.

Library of Congress Catalog Card Number: 88-39742
ISBN: 0-89930-423-0

First published in 1989 by Quorum Books

Greenwood Press, Inc.
88 Post Road West, Westport, Connecticut 06881

Printed in the United States of America

The paper used in this book complies with the
Permanent Paper Standard issued by the National
Information Standards Organization (Z39.48-1984).

10 9 8 7 6 5 4 3 2 1

Copyright Acknowledgments

Grateful appreciation is expressed to the following sources for granting permission to reproduce materials:

Exhibits from *Environmental Tobacco Smoke: Measuring Exposures and Assessing Health Effects*, © 1986 by the National Academy of Sciences. Used with permission.

Extracts from US West Communications (Pacific Northwest Bell) are used with permission from US West Communications.

Extracts from "Creating Your Company Policy" are used courtesy of the American Lung Association.

Extracts from *Model Policy for Smoking in the Workplace* are used with permission from the American Cancer Society, Inc.

Extracts from *Toward a Smoke-Free Work Environment* are used with permission from Smoking Policy Institute, 914 E. Jefferson, Seattle, Washington 98122. (206) 324-4444.

To my wife, Theda, and to my family
Mont, Clark, Laurel, Sally, Rebekah, Ruth,
and Nikolaos.

CONTENTS

EXHIBITS

FOREWORD

Dorothy recently celebrated her fiftieth wedding anniversary. Six years ago, she didn't think she'd make it. Dorothy's right lung had to be removed to excise the cancer that had developed during a lifetime of cigarette smoking. The surgery bought Dorothy more time to enjoy her husband, her children, and grandchildren. Today, however, the cancer has metastasized into her remaining lung, and she may not live to celebrate her next anniversary.

Bob used to sing in the choir. He played one of the three kings in the Christmas pageant and walked triumphantly down the church aisle to the manger scene. Today, suffering from emphysema, he can't take a step without breathing oxygen from a portable tank. Bob also smoked for over forty years. Dorothy and Bob are real people. Their stories represent the tragedy facing thousands of American families; smoking is related to 320,000 deaths each year. One special reason to feel sadness for Dorothy and Bob and their families is that smoking was not yet acknowledged to be "hazardous to your health" when they both got hooked.

Today we know better, and the evidence is overwhelming. It is estimated that cigarette smoking is reponsible for 85 percent of all lung cancer among men and 75 percent among women. Research has shown that smoking is linked to cancers of the mouth, pharynx, larynx, esophagus, pancreas, and bladder. It is a leading cause of heart disease, and it contributes to gastric ulcers, chronic bronchitis, and emphysema.

Since the mid-1960s, the government has tried to educate the American public on the dangers of tobacco use, beginning with the requirement that warning labels appear on all cigarette packages. Moreover, by prohibiting television advertising, the government has endeavored to stem the use of tobacco among impressionable young people. Since 1984, four different labels warn consumers that cigarette smoke contains carbon monoxide; causes cancer, heart disease, and emphysema; complicates pregnancy; and may result in fetal injury, premature birth, and low birth weights. In 1986, warning labels were required for smokeless tobacco products as well.

While individuals may have the right to choose whether or not to smoke, the government does have a responsibility to provide the results of the accumulated research so that their decisions can be informed ones. Additionally, government has a responsibility to protect innocent nonsmokers from the proven menace of secondary smoke. Significant action has included a smoking ban on commercial airline flights of less than two hours and the effort of the General Services Administration to restrict smoking in federal buildings. Employers are increasingly adopting policies aimed at reducing the risks of passive smoking.

Given the warnings of doctors, insurance companies, the American Cancer Society, the American Heart Association, and other experts, the percentage of adults who smoke has decreased from 30 percent in 1985 to 26.5 percent in 1987. This is good news. Perhaps the family, friends, and neighbors of Dorothy and Bob will stop smoking before it is too late.

The sad story is Tom. Not yet 35 years old, Tom has had the benefit of this information, yet he has been smoking since college. What does his future hold? Will he be one of the 40 percent of all adult male smokers who die prematurely? Let's hope Bill Timmins and the wisdom he has offered us in this worthy volume will convince Tom to choose life instead of cigarettes.

Orrin G. Hatch
United States Senator
(R-Utah)

Washington, D.C.
July 1988

Smoking and the Workplace

1

INTRODUCTION

Since Christopher Columbus' first landings in the Americas tobacco has played a prominent role in the history of the Western Hemisphere, and especially of the United States. The "stinking weed" captivated Europe within decades and millions of people, mostly males, became habitual users of tobacco in one or more of its fashionable forms. In time tobacco became an accepted part of life for rich and poor, educated and uneducated, for professors and peasants.

Today, tobacco critics like to say that "the government" would never have tolerated the introduction of such a harmful substance if we had known then what we know now. That is, we now know that smoking is "the most important preventable health problem in the world."[1] Surely, the logic goes, had we understood many years ago the ghastly toll on health and lives taken by tobacco, steps would have been taken by governments everywhere to ban the weed, to outlaw it, to criminalize its growth, possession, and use. Still, nothing like this happened (except in a few isolated incidents), and tens of millions of people smoke, sniff, or chew tobacco products around the world.

In the United States the federal government has actively promoted the use of tobacco products—for generations tobacco growers and producers have greatly benefited from the U.S. Department of Agriculture's tobacco price support system. The tobacco industry in the United States has developed such political clout that it is difficult for anti-smoking groups to counter tobacco's powerful political support. Chapter 2 gives some indication of the size and breadth of this economic impact. Suffice it to say here that we are talking about billions of dollars, millions of jobs, and an economic impact of some magnitude on a majority of the fifty states.

More than a dozen foreign nations ban tobacco advertising and require strong warning labels on tobacco products (as we do in the United States), "but smoking, nevertheless, continues at very high levels, at least among men."[2] The U.S. government continues to spend millions supporting small tobacco farmers and growers and to spend far fewer millions on tobacco-related public health issues—a strange conundrum, at best, trying to correct on one hand the results of what it encourages with the other. Chapter 3 assesses some of these costs to our society and shows how hard it is to measure benefits and costs.

Still, societal attitudes in the United States have changed. Chapter 4 traces some of this shifting in values, especially in recent years. Only middle-aged or older Americans can still remember cigarette advertising where "medical doctors" in white jackets extolled the virtues of one brand of cigarettes over another. Millions can no doubt still recall famous athletes, politicians, singers and performers, movie stars, and scientists who readily posed for tobacco ads (lucrative tobacco promotion contracts were the order of the day). Millions of "doughboys" and "GIs" will always remember the free cigarettes while at war and the smoke breaks on training or field assignments. Airline passengers who flew some years ago will remember when airlines gave out free cigarettes as readily as peanuts or soft drinks are distributed today. It is only comparatively recently that TV and radio advertising of tobacco have been restricted, that threatening warning labels have appeared on packs of cigarettes and in tobacco print advertising, that tobacco has been deglamorized among athletes and performers (and cartoon heroes), and that nonsmokers have asserted their "rights." Suddenly, smokers are a distinctive minority in the United States.

Indeed, as subsequent chapters show, a majority of American companies and more than a third of all government agencies now have nonsmoking policies in the workplace. Nearly three-quarters of the states have passed "clean indoor air acts." Some employers merely restrict smoking to designated places. Many ban it entirely. Some employers won't hire smokers. Some workers are told they cannot smoke on or off the job. Smokers are sometimes told they have no "rights" to smoke, period. And it all appears perfectly legal because it is a health issue, not a religious or civil rights issue at all.[3]

Assuming a company or an agency chooses to implement a nonsmoking policy, Chapter 8 provides numerous guidelines, "next steps," and model policies to make the new nonsmoking policy successful. Chiefly, it means doing your homework first, knowing the mood of your employees (and labor union, if organized), securing top level support, involving smokers and nonsmokers in the developmental stages, and uniform and consistent application and enforcement of the policy thereafter. Surprisingly, few organizations have experienced many problems following such guidelines. Most have experienced significant productivity gains and real cost savings.

Yet smokers remain angry and often unmollified. They can't smoke at all on short flights, they must sit in the last rows on longer flights, smoking is often banned entirely on trains and buses, in many cases they can only smoke outside the office building where they work (even if raining or snowing), they may pay higher insurance premiums, sometimes restaurants can't serve them even if there are empty tables, and so on and on. Many smokers resent the constant efforts to "reform" them. The stage is set for confrontation, litigation, and resentment. Only skilled managers can defuse this potentially explosive and troublesome adversarial relationship.

To top it all off, the U.S. government declares that our nation's official goal is a smokefree society by 2000. Critics see it as unenforceable—a return to the failures of the alcohol prohibition of the 1920s. Others see it as a national policy that is long overdue. Employers must see nonsmoking from a different perspective—healthy employees, a productive workforce, a congenial workplace, and an opportunity to involve everyone in a worthwhile outcome where everyone benefits. That is what this book is all about.

NOTES

1. World Health Organization, *Smoking Control Strategies in Developing Countries* (Geneva: Technical Report Series 695, 1983).

2. William U. Chandler, *Banishing Tobacco* (Worldwatch Institute: Worldwatch Paper 68, January 1986), 29.

3. Surveys show more blacks smoke than whites, however. "The health consequences of cigarette smoking are particularly severe for minorities. . . ." Richard J. Coelho, *Quitting Smoking* (New York: Peter Lang, 1985), 2-3.

2

THE SCOPE
OF THE CONTROVERSY

Tobacco has been part of the history, economics, and romance of the United States since at least Jamestown (the Virginia colony settled in 1607). The success of the tobacco culture and a new method of curing tobacco leaves (which made exporting tobacco profitable) enabled the Virginia colony to survive. From 1616 on, tobacco flourished as an agricultural product in the South. It is no exaggeration to say that billions of pounds of tobacco were grown and exported over the next 300 years, creating millions of jobs and making tobacco the second most important crop of the South, other than "King Cotton." The tobacco leaf was prominent as an illustration on colonial paper money, was featured on millions of tax and revenue stamps, on buildings and architectural renderings, and so forth. Tobacco influenced in part the southern plantation system, the slave trade, reconstruction, and the economic recovery of the South, from the Civil War through the New Deal. Tobacco, however, helped deplete the soil and and required enormous continuous investments in soil stabilization, growing, curing, and marketing to keep its place in the economic structure of the South. Tobacco stimulated a rich literature—from *Gone with the Wind* to *Song of the South* to *Tobacco Road*. The romance of Mississippi River steamboating is tied up with the tobacco story. Poetry, plays, movies, novels, theatre, and politics of the South and the nation have been inextricably bound up with tobacco. Some of the classic tobacco brand symbols are part of the early American romance with cigarettes, cigars, and other tobacco products—the camel on Camel brand cigarettes, the Lucky Strike pack, the Philip Morris bellboy, and so on. These advertising images are presented in some detail in Hal Morgan, *Symbols of America*. Great universities, research institutes, family dynasties, museums, and galleries have all profited from the billions of dollars flowing from the sale of the tobacco leaf. Few agricultural products have ever played a more prominent role in nearly every aspect of the social, economic, and political life of the country and a region. Yet tobacco has been a mixed blessing. It made billions of dollars—but it has cost billions. Millions of people have enjoyed the products made from the tobacco leaf, but more millions have objected to its smell and byproducts. Millions of people have found employment in the tobacco industry, but many thousands claim their lives and careers have been blighted by its health effects. Tobacco has influenced courts, capitals, and congresses as one of the most powerful lobbies in the United States. Truly, tobacco has been a prominent part of America's history.

In 1983 Chase Econometrics of Bala Cynwyd, Pennsylvania, conducted an analysis of the tobacco industry in the United States to "determine the economic impact of the industry on the domestic economy." Among the major findings of the Chase Econometrics study, volume 1, were:[1]

- Tobacco excise and sales tax payments of $9.79 billion were paid to federal, state, and local governments. This represented 34.6 percent of total consumer expenditures on tobacco products.

- Including excise and sales taxes along with income and corporate profit taxes, the tobacco core sectors paid out more than $13.46 billion in federal, state, and local taxes. This represented 47.6 percent of total consumer expenditures on tobacco products.

- The tobacco core sectors employed more than 414,000 persons during 1983 and paid compensation totaling more than $6.72 billion.

- Supplier industries produced more than $30.3 billion in goods and services to meet the production requirements of the tobacco core sectors.

- The supplier industries employed 296,000 workers and paid out almost $7.4 billion in compensation.

- Combined, the tobacco core sectors and supplier industries accounted for $31.5 billion of GNP in 1983 and employed 710,00 workers to produce and deliver tobacco products and their associated goods and services.

- To meet the consumption demands of workers and their families affected by the tobacco industry, 1.59 million workers were employed to produce the necessary goods and services in all business sectors, which accounted for $50.6 billion of GNP.

Volume 2 of the Chase study addressed "The Impacts on the State Economies" and concluded:[2]

- Nationally, 414,000 persons were employed as a result of the production and distribution activities of the tobacco core sector. These workers received $6.75 billion in total compensation. On a regional basis the employment impacts ranged from a high of 73,740 workers in the tobacco-producing state of North Carolina to a low of 447 jobs in Alaska. North Carolina also had the highest compensation impact of $1.5 billion, but Alaska with its high wage structure reflecting its high cost of living ranked forty-sixth with $9.0 million. The lowest compensation impact occurred in Wyoming with $5.9 million.

- Generally, the largest employment impacts occurred in the tobacco growing and processing region of the United States, which is the southeastern portion of the United States, most specifically the states of North Carolina, Kentucky, and Virginia. Combined, these three states accounted for 39 percent of the tobacco core sector's total employment impact and 45 percent of the total compensation impact. Georgia and Tennessee also experienced significant primary impacts from the core and supplier sectors.

- States with very large population bases and thus a large source of demand for tobacco products also displayed relatively large total employment and compensation impacts. These employment and income opportunities were primarily generated within the wholesale and retail trade sectors. Such states were California, New York, and Texas. Combined, these three states accounted for 14 percent of the tobacco core sector's employment impact and 15 percent of the compensation impact.

- The distribution of the tobacco core sector's employment and compensation inputs across the remaining states primarily reflects the distribution of population and, more specifically, cigarette sales across states.

Obviously tobacco plays a big economic role nationally and in many of the states. In many local areas and regions tobacco is the primary industry—the chief source of jobs and family well-being. This economic clout cannot be dismissed easily.

Still, in recent years tobacco and smoking have become ever more controversial. The surgeon general of the United States condemned smoking in an initial report to Congress in the 1960s, and other critical reports have followed. Since 1970 a warning statement has appeared on every package of cigarettes. Beginning with the Comprehensive Education Act (Public Law 98-474) of 1984, cigarette packs and advertising must reproduce four new health warnings, to be rotated quarterly. The incumbent surgeon general, C. Everett Koop, has said:[3]

In May 1984, I threw down a challenge to the physicians, other health providers, and all citizens of our country. I said that I truly believed it is possible for us to attain a smoke-free society in the United States by the year 2000, and I asked them to join me in reaching for this goal. I said that it was something that ought to be done, something that could be done, and something I believe will be done.

Today, I am more confident than ever. I base this feeling, more than on anything else, on the enthusiastic, positive response I have received from my fellow physicians in hundreds of letters, telephone calls, and personal meetings. . . .

No one is suggesting that physicians alone can bring about a smoke-free society by the year 2000. We must have help—help from our voluntary health agencies, our hospital administrators, our schools, our public health people, and, not least, from the American Medical Association and its constituent organizations. What is needed is a total package of motivation, education, and training efforts. With such a package, we can reach our goal of a smoke-free society.

The Tobacco Institute, a trade association for the cigarette companies objects to this strident call. They see this "smokeless society" effort as an "attempt to introduce, under the varying guises of 'science,' an objective value standard, one that 'should' be imposed on all persons." Further, the Tobacco Institute, represented by Professor James A. Buchanan (the founder of the "public choice movement" and winner of the Nobel Prize in economics in 1986) has argued:[4]

There is an implicit recognition by all parties here that, although each may have preferences over the others' behavior, any attempt to *impose* one person's preferences on the behavior of another must be predicted to set off reciprocal attempts to have one's own behavior constrained in a like fashion. An attitude of "live and let live," or mutual tolerance and mutual respect, may be better for all of us, despite the occasional deviance from ordinary standards of common decency.

Buchanan then continued with a precise definition of the pro-smoking position on freedom to choose:

Such an attitude would seem to be that of anyone who claimed to hold to democratic and individualistic values, in which each person's preferences are held to count equally with those of others. By contrast, the genuine elitist, who somehow thinks that his or her own preferences are "superior to," "better than" or "more correct" than those of others, will, of course, try to control the behavior of everyone else, while holding fast to his or her own liberty to do as he or she pleases.

For those who wish to review the scientific evidence against tobacco smoke (or, the lack of evidence as the case may be) from a perspective other than the Tobacco Institute, readers are referred to the recent work of the Committee on Passive Smoking, Board on Environmental Studies and Toxicology, of the National Research Council (established in 1916 by the National Academy of

Sciences under its congressional charter of 1863), *Environmental Tobacco Smoke: Measuring Exposures and Assessing Health Effects.* The committee "restricted itself to analysis of the scientific data" and sought to "prepare a scientifically responsible report" (p. vi).

Despite rebuttals by the Tobacco Institute, many Americans seem to have been alarmed by the government-required warnings, the negative statistics so widely promulgated, and changes in society's attitudes toward smoking (see Chapter 4). Consumption of tobacco is down and the number of users has declined steadily since the first reports on smoking by the surgeon general and other health groups.

Exhibit 2.1 shows the trend in cigarette consumption between 1955 and 1985 for males and females.[5] It shows a reduction of almost one-third in male smokers since the first *Surgeon General's Report on Smoking and Health* in 1964. The percentage of smokers in the general population increased steadily from 1900 to about 1964. Today about the same percentage of males and females smoke. Exhibit 2.2 shows U.S. cigarette consumption from 1900 to 1985. As the National Research Council concluded, "the general probability

Exhibit 2.1
Percentage of Current Smokers in the United States. Adult Population, by Sex, 1955-1983

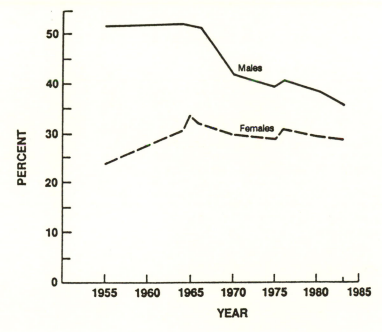

Exhibit 2.2

U.S. Cigarette Consumption, 1900 to 1985[a]

Year	Total Billions	Number Per Capita, 18 Years and Older	Year	Total Billions	Number Per Capita, 18 Years and Older	Year	Total Billions	Number Per Capita, 18 Years and Older
1900	2.5	54	1930	119.3	1,485	1960	484.4	4,171
1901	2.5	53	1931	114.0	1,399	1961	502.5	4,266
1902	2.8	60	1932	102.8	1,245	1962	508.4	4,265
1903	3.1	64	1933	111.6	1,334	1963	523.9	4,345
1904	3.3	66	1934	125.7	1,483	1964	511.3	4,195
1905	3.6	70	1935	134.4	1,564	1965	528.8	4,259
1906	4.5	86	1936	152.7	1,754	1966	541.3	4,287
1907	5.3	99	1937	162.8	1,847	1967	549.3	4,280
1908	5.7	105	1938	163.4	1,830	1968	545.6	4,186
1909	7.0	125	1939	172.1	1,900	1969	528.9	3,993
1910	8.6	151	1940	181.9	1,976	1970	536.5	3,985
1911	10.1	173	1941	208.9	2,236	1971	555.1	4,037
1912	13.2	223	1942	245.0	2,585	1972	566.8	4,043
1913	15.8	260	1943	284.3	2,956	1973	589.7	4,148
1914	16.5	267	1944	296.3	3,039	1974	599.0	4,141
1915	17.9	285	1945	340.6	3,449	1975	607.2	4,123
1916	25.2	395	1946	344.3	3,446	1976	613.5	4,092
1917	35.7	551	1947	345.4	3,416	1977	617.0	4,051˙
1918	45.6	697	1948	358.9	3,505	1978	616.0	3,967
1919	48.0	727	1949	360.9	3,480	1979	621.5	3,861
1920	44.6	665	1950	369.8	3,522	1980	631.5	3,851
1921	50.7	742	1951	397.1	3,744	1981	640.0	3,840
1922	53.4	770	1952	416.0	3,886	1982	634.0	3,753
1923	64.4	911	1953	408.2	3,778	1983	600.0	3,502
1924	71.0	982	1954	387.0	3,546	1984	600.4[b]	3,461[b]
1925	79.8	1,085	1955	396.4	3,597	1985	595.0[c]	3,384[c]
1926	89.1	1,191	1956	406.5	3,650			
1927	97.5	1,279	1957	422.5	3,755			
1928	106.0	1,366	1958	448.9	3,953			
1929	118.6	1,504	1959	467.5	4,073			

[a]Includes overseas forces, 1917–1919 and 1940 to date. Commodity Economics Division, Economic Research Service, USDA.

[b]Subject to revision.

[c]Estimated.

SOURCE: U.S. Department of Agriculture, 1985.

of being exposed to some [secondhand smoke] for the nonsmoker has increased until quite recently."

Exhibit 2.3 shows that total cigarette consumption has not declined as rapidly as the percentage of people who smoke. See also Exhibit 2.4 for total U.S. consumption of cigars and tobacco for pipes and "loose" tobacco consumption (hand-rolled cigarettes). While per capita U.S. consumption of cigarettes has declined, these figures are averages over the total U.S. population, including smokers and nonsmokers. Among smokers, daily cigarette consumption has actually increased. Smokers have tended to become

Exhibit 2.3
Total Cigarette Consumption (Domestic Sales), 1955-1985

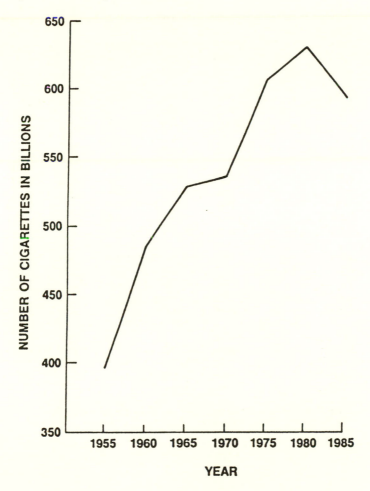

Exhibit 2.4

U.S. Consumption of Cigars and Tobacco for Pipes and
Hand-rolled Cigarettes

Year	Cigars, millions	Tobacco, Mn. lb[a]	Year	Cigars, millions	Tobacco, Mn. lb[a]	Year	Cigars, millions
1920	8,609	—	1950	5,608	104.3	1980	5,386
1921	7,435	—	1951	5,778	97.4	1981	5,231
1922	7,527	—	1952	6,037	92.9	1982	4,901
1923	7,505	—	1953	6,107	84.3	1983	4,884
1924	7,189	—	1954	6,024	81.2		
1925	6,949	—	1955	6,078	77.8		
1926	7,008	—	1956	6,039	70.0		
1927	7,008	—	1957	6,194	68.9		
1928	6,874	—	1958	6,586	74.4		
1929	6,972	—	1959	7,377	71.9		
1930	6,272	—	1960	7,434	72.2		
1931	5,656	—	1961	7,083	72.7		
1932	4,724	—	1962	7,103	69.8		
1933	4,553	—	1963	7,434	69.7		
1934	4,818	—	1964	9,899	81.7		
1935	4,943	—	1965	8,949	69.8		
1936	5,362	—	1966	8,610	68.6		
1937	5,516	—	1967	8,403	66.4		
1938	5,294	—	1968	8,331	69.6		
1939	5,469	—	1969	8,579	68.3		
1940	5,491	—	1970	8,881	74.0		
1941	5,933	—	1971	8,830	69.5		
1942	6,339	—	1972	11,125	66.8		
1943	5,350	—	1973	11,126	59.5		
1944	4,878	—	1974	9,339			
1945	5,027	—	1975	8,663			
1946	5,929	—	1976	7,492			
1947	5,706	—	1977	6,792			
1948	5,860	—	1978	6,231			
1949	5,625	—	1979	5,706			

[a]Tobacco for pipes and hand-rolled cigarettes, not available prior to 1950.

"heavier" smokers, while "light" smokers seem to have given up the habit. This may make efforts at smoking cessation by companies and government agencies more difficult since many smokers who were "easy quitters" have already kicked their addiction and habit (see chapter 5 for smoking cessation programs of the American Lung Association, American Cancer Society, and others).

Considerable research shows that most smokers in the United States begin in their early teens, especially among males. Smoking is still perceived by many youth as "adult" behavior and a "rite of passage into manhood." Long years of smoking mean the addiction is more severe and the habit more ingrained—thus more difficult to break. A number of other demographic data are obvious: "There is an inverse relationship between educational level and smoking in the United States. Smoking has come to symbolize the opposite of fashion, status, and upward mobility." Nonsmoking programs designed by well-educated, white collar managers will likely have more difficulties than cessation programs where blue collar and pink collar and union worker input is secured early in the process. In fact, there is some evidence that blacks smoke more than whites. So, "white male executives can puff away in their private offices but the black clerical staff, being in the open areas covered by [a] smoking ban, must put out their cigarettes. Therefore, the 'rights' of blacks are being disproportionately affected." In at least some cases (especially New York City) black leaders and the Tobacco Institute have tried to turn "indoor smoking into a civil rights issue." Not all black leadership have responded this way—the "NAACP as a group has remained officially neutral."[7]

Clearly, tobacco plays a powerful role in the U.S. economy and society. But the industry and the habit are under attack and losing some ground for the first time since the colonial era.

NOTES

1. Chase Econometrics, *The Economic Impact of the Tobacco Industry on the United States Economy in 1983: The Impacts on the National Economy*, vol. 1, 1-1–1-2. Some of tobacco's history in the United States is found in John D. Hicks, *The Federal Union* (Cambridge, Mass.: Riverside Press, 1952), 23-24, 39, 41, 52-53, 513.

2. Chase Econometrics, volume 2: *The Impacts on the State Economies*, 1-2, 1-4.

3. C. Everett Koop, "Is a Smokeless Society by 2000 Achievable?" *Archives of Internal Medicine* 145 (September 1985): 1581.

4. James M. Buchanan, "Politics and Meddlesome Preferences," in Robert D. Tollison, ed., *Clearing the Air: Perspectives on Environmental Tobacco Smoke* (Lexington, Mass.: Lexington Books, 1988), 107-115. The Appendix (119-144) methodically seeks to repudiate most of the scientific case against smoking.

5. These four exhibits are taken from National Research Council, *Environmental Tobacco Smoke: Measuring Exposures and Health Effects* (Washington, D.C.: National Academy Press, 1986), 16-19 (references on page 21 of this book for exact table and figure sources).

6. William U. Chandler, *Banishing Tobacco* (Worldwatch Institute: Worldwatch Paper 68, January 1986), 11.

7. Susan Milligan, "Eyes on the Lies," *Washington Monthly* 19 (June 1987): 39-42. See also a related story of racism in a suit against American Brands, Inc. The tobacco company spent an estimated $10 million on the trial. Much of the criticism of the case hinged on the charge that "it was more a case of blacks against whites" than the plaintiff against a tobacco company. Scott Ticer, "This Tobacco Case Hardly Clears the Air," *Business Week* (March 7, 1988): 76, 78.

3

THE COSTS OF SMOKING

Tobacco is a filthy weed,
That from the devil does proceed;
It drains your purse, it burns your clothes.
And makes a chimney of your nose.
                    —Oliver Wendell Holmes

The Tobacco Institute, the trade association for U.S. cigarette manufacturers, has long criticized scientific studies attacking smoking, including the surgeon general's reports, and argued that the statistics are faulty, the research findings are questionable, and the conclusions are wrong or, at least, not supported by the data. The cost figures used by anti-smoking groups are particularly specious, according to the Tobacco Institute.

The Tobacco Institute spends a lot of money supporting smokers' rights and opposing bans, restrictions, and litigation. Two figures illustrate this "muscle" or financial strength—tobacco companies "spend about $1.5 billion annually promoting their products. By contrast, the budget of the U.S. Office on Smoking and Health is just $3.5 million a year."[1] In New Jersey it is alleged that a lobbyist for "five tobacco companies spent nearly $1 million on lobbying and campaign contributions" to soften an anti-smoking bill before the state legislature (one local legislative leader alone received $12,000 from one tobacco firm to assist his election).[2]

When the surgeon general says that cigarettes kill young smokers (by shortening their lives), tobacco proponents have said that "war kills young people." The *Harvard Medical School Health Letter*, however, refutes that by converting deaths from war and deaths from tobacco usage to "years of life" lost from each.[3] Harvard's *Health Letter* states that war-related deaths in recent decades in the United States cost about 3 million "years of life," but cigarettes have taken well over 30 million "years of life" in the same period. There are obviously a lot of ways to die, many of which are unavoidable. Still, cigarette smoking "has been identified as the chief avoidable cause of death in the United States." The *Journal of the American Medical Association* estimates tobacco-caused deaths at over 320,000 annually.[4]

The Worldwatch Institute in Washington, D.C., says that "almost one-fifth of all U.S. deaths can be traced to cigarette smoke," or 375,000 deaths. Worldwatch says that, coupled with lost work from smoking-related illnesses this costs the United States between $27 billion and $61 billion per year (or, as much as $3.15 per pack of cigarettes smoked). This figure does not include the approximate $30 billion annual cost of the tobacco itself. Worldwatch also estimates smoking wastes 7 percent of a smoker's time on the job. Each smoker, therefore, costs an employer $650 extra in insurance and cleanup costs. In rebuttal, the Tobacco Institute charges these figures are "fanciful extrapolations that have very little to do with hard, factual data."[5]

Whatever the actual figure, these deaths represent an annual loss of life greater than World War I, the Korean conflict, and the Vietnam conflict combined. Dr. Jonathan Fielding estimates smoking is responsible for fully half of all mortality caused by fire (1,500 lives lost per year, 4,000 injuries)—that is, deaths in apartment fires caused by smoking equal 38 percent; hotel and motel fire deaths from smoking equal 32 percent; mobile homes, 23 percent; residential, 21 percent; and private dwellings, 17 percent. Fielding estimates every nonsmoker pays $100 annually for medical care for smoking-induced illness (paid largely through taxes and health insurance premiums). Fielding's article cites eighty-seven sources—readers are encouraged to check his sources (they are credible, defensible, and thorough).[6]

Dr. Walter Willett and his coauthors have compared risks of coronary heart disease between males and females. They report that:[7]

We prospectively examined the incidence of coronary heart disease in relation to cigarette smoking in a cohort of 119,404 female nurses who were 30 to 55 years of age in 1976 and were free of diagnosed coronary disease. During six years of follow-up, 65 of the women died of fatal coronary heart disease and 242 had a nonfatal myocardial infarction.

The number of cigarettes smoked per day was positively associated with the risk of fatal coronary heart disease (relative risk = 5.5 for > 25 cigarettes per day), nonfatal myocardial infarction (relative risk = 5.8), and angina pectoris (relative risk = 2.6).

Even smoking 1 to 4 or 5 to 14 cigarettes per day was associated with a twofold to threefold increase in the risk of fatal coronary heart disease or nonfatal infarction. Overall, cigarette smoking accounted for approximately half these events. The attributable (absolute excess) risk of coronary heart disease due to current smoking was highest among women who were already at increased risk because of older age, a parental history of myocardial infarction, a higher relative weight, hypertension, hypercholesterolemia, or diabetes. In contrast, former smokers had little, if any, increase in risk.

These prospective data emphasize the importance of cigarette smoking as a determinant of coronary heart disease in women, as well as the markedly increased hazards associated with this habit in combination with other risk factors for this disease.

The Tobacco Institute rebuts such data by pointing out that 90 percent of smokers do not have heart attacks, cancer, or other health problems, and that the conclusions drawn simply aren't justified by the data.

Robert D. Tollison, professor at George Mason University, edited a text in 1986 called *Smoking and Society: Toward a More Balanced Assessment.* The research was supported by "a number of tobacco companies." Tollison himself says "the public debate about smoking has been remarkably one-sided." Tollison insists that typical studies on smoking give only the costs but "neglect the benefit side of the account." He states that people (millions of them) willingly purchase and use tobacco products. The price of tobacco products (hundreds of millions of dollars) "reflects the value of the resources used to produce them" and, simply, "users obtain benefits from tobacco products equal to their expenditures on these items." This is pure economics —and Tollison states that the debate over the "costs" of tobacco is unbalanced because of faulty analysis and opponents' constant refusal to consider user "benefits" in their analysis (see pages 3 to 14 of Tollison's work).

Part 4 of Tollison's book addresses "Smoking: The Context of the Economy." Some of the co-authors in this section address questions such as the impact of tobacco on the national economy. They conclude that "the tobacco industry turns out to be a relatively small sector in terms of its share of national output and employment, but a very large factor in tax collection at both the federal and state/local levels" (253). Other writers address the "costs" of the "litter" left by smokers and conclude that "any argument against smoking on this ground would apply with much greater force to many food products" (278). What about the "costs" of smoke breaks taken by smokers? If wages are paid according to output, "Any loss in output is reflected in a lower wage," so this is a cost "borne directly by the smoker" and is not a true societal cost (278). Another writer persuasively argues that severe restrictions on tobacco advertising "should not exceed those reasonably applying to other products and services" 309-32). A bill now before the U.S. Congress would ban *all* print advertising for tobacco products—ads were restricted in 1971 from radio and television by the federal regulatory agency involved.

In his concluding remarks (343-45) Tollison says, "Everyone finds certain activities of others bothersome," but heavy-handed government regulation is certainly not the solution. "Thus," Tollison writes, "both smokers and non-smokers should be alert to what the anti-smoking crusade represents: nothing more and nothing less than an assault on individual liberty." That "cost" he feels, far outweighs the alleged "benefits" of the anti-smoking campaign.

Even William F. Buckley, Jr., has argued that "it pays to remind ourselves that the most important things of all are up to the individual . . ." and that the government should not be called on to "tell us how much, or whether, we can smoke, drink, etc." See his essay, "The Weed," reprinted in *The Tobacco Industry in Transition*.

Beyond deaths and statistics on lost "years of life," smoking has been charged with costing companies and government agencies a great deal of money. Some of these tobacco-related costs may be surprising because they may not be anticipated by employers. Obviously, most companies *do* feel smoking costs their company money.

The American Management Society published a "1988 AMS Smoking Policies Survey" comparing results with 1986 results and reported that companies felt the costs of employee smoking were significant, as shown in Exhibit 3.1.[8]

What are some of these "costs"? One interesting example is the problem of smokers who exhale particulate matter for as much as an hour after

Exhibit 3.1
Survey: Does Smoking Increase Company Costs?

COST	percent answering "yes"	1986 percent	1986 rank
Medical care/insurance premiums	69%	65%	1
Absenteeism	45%	38%	2
Maintenance costs	43%	39%	3
Accidents	11%	11%	4
No effect on costs	20%	24%	

smoking—no small problem for companies that must maintain "clean rooms." Companies and government research labs involved in work with pharmaceuticals, computer chips, and other products must provide costly air filtration systems, face masks, "bunny suits," and so on. Research demonstrates smokers exhale considerable particulate matter—dangerous to product purity, air integrity, and so forth. The research suggests smokers should go through a mouth-cleansing exercise after smoking, before returning to the "clean room."[9]

Other research demonstrates secondhand tobacco smoke ("passive smoke") harms computer hardware—requiring more frequent cleaning of the machines, a higher repair ratio, and so on. The evidence suggests persons in data processing may wish to ban smoking from computer rooms, as much for the "health" of the hardware and software as for that of employees: chips run hotter than normal, disc drives crash, machines require more service, and other problems occur.[10]

The Tobacco Institute publicly favors restricting smoking to designated rooms or areas, rather than outright bans. But setting up separate rooms designated for smoking can prove very expensive. For instance, setting up specific smoking rooms, improving ventilation systems, and trying to ensure smoke does not drift back into nonsmoking areas can be costly; examples show costs from $5,000 to $80,000 per room. Texas Instruments spent over $500,000 "trying to retrofit its buildings" but did not solve the problem. Companies would have to replace "the volume of air in affected rooms about 250 times more often than it normally is replaced—measures that would increase heating, cooling, and air pumping costs 250-fold.[11]

Salt Lake County (Utah) recently built an enormous new county government complex, partly designed to solve the smoke recirculation problem (smoking was restricted to a few designated areas). Despite an air filtering and circulation system specifically designed with the smoking issue in mind, after less than a year of experience, nonsmokers have complained so often of recirculating tobacco smoke that county officials finally banned smoking throughout the building.

As documented in some of the cases in Chapters 6 and 7, smoke tends to be drawn back into ventilation systems regardless of earnest efforts to prevent it. Still, the Tobacco Institute says other pollutants, not merely cigarette smoke, cause poor air quality. The Tobacco Institute reports government tests "revealed that 98 percent of air quality complaints were traced to bad ventilation, dirt and bacteria."[12]

Some of the costs of smoking may be counted as individual or personal costs that ought not to be included in overall societal calculations. For instance, May Hayes wrote in *Personnel Administrator* that "I am not defending the habit of smoking. It's indefensible."[13] Still, she appeals to nonsmokers to acknowledge that smoking is an addiction and hard to quit (she's tried, "many times"). She lists costs such as annoying coughs, holes "burned in our clothes, in our furniture, in our cars," burned fingers, weight gains when smokers stop, tobacco breath, and so on. Still she asks nonsmokers to "stop trying to reform us."

Some significant smoking-related costs can be more easily calculated, however. For instance, auto accident rates for smokers are significantly higher than nonsmokers—due to distractions such as lighting up, flicking ashes, smoke haze on inside windshields, smoke in the eyes, and so on.[14]

Around the United States are various businesses that have seen costs drop sharply when smoking is totally banned. Some hotels and motels, freestanders and chains, are banning smoking entirely, or setting aside a block of non-smoking rooms (see Chapter 7 for examples). For instance, Lyndon Sanders runs "Non-Smokers Inn" in Dallas, Texas. He says "It costs me $2,400 per year more in cleaning costs and lost productivity due to absenteeism to employ a smoker." The 135-room motel is quite profitable—he employs no smokers. Sanders adds a $250 cleaning fee if a guest breaks the rules and smokes in a room.[15]

Many other costs of smoking at work can be calculated—cleaning up offices (ash trays, desk burns, soiled drapes, dirty air filters, carpet damage). Down time for smokers (more frequent breaks and longer breaks) is discussed in later chapters. Just the "routine" of smoking is a time waster (tamping, lighting up, dropping the ashes).

The National Public Employer Labor Relations Association reported the costs of smoking as follows.[16]

It costs employers an average of $4,600 more per year to keep a smoker, rather than a nonsmoker, on the average payroll. The cost breakdown is as follows:

- $1,820 in lost productivity. This represents thirty minutes a day for smoking breaks and smoking rituals such as lighting up and puffing.
- $1,000 in damage from cigarette burns and extra cleaning maintenance for smoke pollution.
- $765 in lost time due to the average smoker's increased chance of illness and early death.
- $230 in medical care. Heavy smokers use health care at least 80 percent more than nonsmokers.
- $220 in absenteeism. Smokers are absent 50 percent more often than nonsmokers (or nearly 2.2 days more per year).

- $86 for the effect of smoking on the health of nonsmokers working nearby.

- $45 for accidents due to loss of attention, eye irritation, coughing, and so forth.

- $45 in increased fire insurance.

The Smoking Policy Institute of Seattle, Washington—one of the foremost groups in the country at assisting companies to implement nonsmoking programs—has elaborated on the above kinds of cost figures by noting that: (1) Boeing (in Seattle) could have saved $50 million by a complete ban on workplace smoking; (2) Unigard Insurance in Seattle saved $6,000 a year in cleaning service charges after installing a nonsmoking policy; and (3) giant Weyerhaeuser estimated the costs of smoking at its corporate headquarters at more than $4.9 million per year. Obviously the Tobacco Institute would repudiate these figures—or at least any generalizations drawn from them—as fanciful extrapolations and not based on hard data. The Tobacco Institute's research position is ably presented in a new text, *Clearing the Air*, where the authors attempt to repudiate nearly every scientific study on smoking to date.[17]

Still, the Worldwatch Institute flatly states, "smokers cost employers money."[18] They list as "costs" inefficiency, ill health, added insurance costs, additional cleanup costs, reduced nonsmokers' morale, and others. William L. Weis and Bruce W. Miller have addressed these employer costs in much more detail.[19] They report studies that absenteeism is significantly higher among smokers; that productivity is lower among smokers ("smokers waste time"); that the costs of health and fire insurance are much higher where smokers are involved; that maintenance costs can be much lower with nonsmoking policies (less damage to equipment and furniture, lower redecorating costs, lower ventilation costs); that the effects of "passive smoke" on co-workers results in numerous complaints, annoyances, and costs for medical care ("eye irritation seems to be the main complaint"), along with "psychological harm" to employee morale and nonsmoker "frustration."

From a typical nonsmoker's view the costs of passive smoking are high. To a typical smoker, the costs of heavy-handed regulation are unacceptable. To a majority of U.S. companies (and more than one-third of government agencies), restrictions or bans on smoking are based upon cost-benefit analysis that shows smoking costs the employer money in terms of employee health and productivity.

Perhaps the highest cost, other than loss of human life and health, of course, is that of confrontational and adversarial relationships that have become characteristic of the smoking/nonsmoking debate in recent years. Cooperation has become confrontation. Attempts at humor have become heavy with sarcasm ("O.K. to inhale your cigarette but don't exhale"). Co-workers who tolerated one another now act as adversaries. Reprisal and "getting even" have become more commonplace. As one writer stated it, "Most people agree smoking in the workplace is a touchy issue that, when pushed to legal limits, could destroy friendships, create enemies and subsequently disrupt job performance."[20]

Countless examples of challenges to "rights" can be cited—grievances filed against a co-worker, quarrels and fighting between parties at either extreme, aggravation taking bizarre forms of response. One critic of a local nonsmoking ordinance (a smoker) said, "I can see an ordinance like this running one of two ways: it'll either become unenforceable or extremely expensive to enforce."[21]

This breakdown in collegiality among co-workers is a cost. Managers will do well to follow the suggestions in Chapter 8 when an organization chooses to implement a nonsmoking policy. Morale, productivity, and the "bottom line" all suffer when co-workers become adversaries over a habit like smoking.

NOTES

1. James E. Peters, "The No Smoking Controversy Heats Up," *Restaurant Business* 85 (September 29, 1986): 122.

2. Lawrence J. Tell, "A Loophole Burns Cigarette Foes," *Legal Affairs* (March 7, 1988): 78.

3. "Cigarettes: Prevention or Cure?" *Harvard Medical School Health Letter* 10 (March 1985): 3-5.

4. *Journal of the American Medical Association* 258 (November 20, 1987), pp. 2648, 2652 (this figure represents 15.7 percent of all U.S. deaths, says JAMA). See also a major work on passive smoking in National Research Council, *Environmental Tobacco Smoke* (Washington, D.C.: National Academy Press, 1986).

5. William U. Chandler, *Banishing Tobacco,* Worldwatch Paper 68 (January 1986), 5-47; also, Janet Ralof, "An Economic Case for Banning Smoking," *Science News* 129 (January 18, 1986): 40.

6. Jonathan E. Fielding, "Smoking: Health Effects and Control," *The New England Journal of Medicine* 313 (August 22, 1985): 494-98.

7. Walter C. Willett et al., "Relative and Absolute Excess Risks of Coronary Heart Disease among Women Who Smoke Cigarettes," *New England Journal of Medicine* 317 (November 19, 1987): 1303-09.

8. See Table 2 in "The Smoking Controversy Goes to Court," *Management World* 17 (January/February 1988): 13.

9. "Heavy Breathing," *Scientific American* 266 (October 1986): 91.

10. Mary Miles, "Smokeout in the Office," *Computer Decisions* 17 (December 3, 1985): 70.

11. James Braham, "Ban It or Restrict It?" *Industry Week* 235 (November 30,

1987): 17. See also Ralof, "An Economic Case," 40, and Miles, "Smokeout in the Office," 70.

12. "Smokeout Spurs Tobacco Institute to Offer a Challenge of Its Own," *United States Tobacco and Candy Journal* 214 (December 28, 1987): 3, 10.

13. "A Fire on One end and a Fool on the Other," *Personnel Administrator* 30 (March 1985): 28, 30, 31. The quote "A fire on one end . . ." is actually from New York Tribune editor Horace Greeley of the mid-1850s. See also Russell Baker, "A Smoking Aftermath," *The New York Times Magazine* 134 (April 21, 1985): 20, for a satirical view of such costs by an ex-smoker.

14. Monica Gonzales, "Smoking down the Highway," *American Demographics* 10 (January 1988): 20.

15. Ibid., "No Smoke Inn."

16. National Public Employer Labor Relations Association, *Newsletter* 8 (January 31, 1986): 6.

17. See Robert D. Tollison, ed., *Clearing the Air: Perspectives on Environmental Tobacco Smoke* (Lexington, Mass.: D. C. Heath and Company, 1988). See also Tobacco Institute, *The Economic Impact of the Tobacco Industry on the United States Economy: Executive Summary* (Chase Econometrics, 1984).

18. Chandler, *Banishing Tobacco*, 33-34.

19. William L. Weis and Bruce W. Miller, *The Smoke-free Workplace* (Buffalo: Prometheus Books, 1985), 15-69.

20. Kris Aaron, "Smoking Ordinance Sparks Feud," *Phoenix Business Journal* (March 25, 1985): 1, 7.

21. Ibid., 1. See also Nancy R. Gibbs, "All Fired Up over Smoking," *Time* 13 (April 18, 1988): 64-73.

4

THE CHANGING ATTITUDES
OF SOCIETY

Perhaps nothing better illustrates the changing attitude of U.S. society toward smoking than the fall 1986 issue of *Army Reserve* 23: 12-15. This is the official magazine of the U.S. Army Reserve. The article reproduces one of Bill Mauldin's classic "Willie and Joe" GI cartoons from 1944. The cartoon characters both have lighted cigarettes dangling from their mouths—as common a scene in the "old" Army as imaginable. The caption of the accompanying 1986 story, however, reads, "What's Wrong with This Picture? 'Smoke 'em if you got 'em' is no longer part of the Army's lingo." The issue then devotes the next three pages to describing the new "U.S. Army Smoking Policy," which is described as "the end of an era." Millions of veterans from World War I, World War II, Korea, and Vietnam will remember the free cigarettes on the battlefield, butt cans (and policing parade grounds and barracks), and stopping training for a smoke. But no more. Smoking is "out" in the Army, and the new motto is "Combat-ready soldiers don't smoke." Smoking is banned in combat training and advanced individual training; the Army offers smoking cessation programs, has designated restricted smoking areas in Army buildings, and bans smoking in military vehicles. "Role models" will be educated to influence soldiers not to smoke. An Army representative was asked "What articles of the Uniform Code of Military Justice could apply to violators?" The official answer:

Army policy limits the use of Uniform Code of Military Justice punishment to violations of lawful orders (Article 92) that demonstrate a willful disregard for the health and comfort of non-smokers. We expect such cases to be few and far between, as almost all violations can best be handled with an on-the-spot correction.

Older veterans are amazed to see the de-emphasis on tobacco products at post commissaries and exchanges, in boot camp, and throughout the military. The smoking picture has certainly changed in the armed forces.

There was a time in recent years that executives and managers often smoked at least partly because it was manly, created an aura, and was part of the proper image the upwardly mobile professional wanted to project. Pipes, cigars, and aromatic cigarettes were trendy, "in," and "with it." This image, too, appears to have changed radically. Indeed, a headline in *Executive Fitness* 19 (June 1988) reads, "Warning: Smoking Can Be Hazardous to Your Career." The feature story says nonsmokers are much more likely to hold top jobs in a company—indeed, the article reports 61 percent of top executives have quit the habit and now seem to favor nonsmokers. The feature describes why smoking is "becoming a danger to your career," in terms of fitness, costs, productivity, and corporate image. And "it's only going to get rougher" on smokers, the piece concludes, saying, "smokers do not have rights."

For many decades tobacco ads have displayed attractive people smoking— obviously to link good looks with smoking or the use of other tobacco products. There was a time when smoking was seen as sexy or glamorous. But a paper presented in 1988 at the ninth annual meeting of the Society of Behavioral Medicine (in Boston) refutes that image.[1]

Despite advertisements that portray smokers as glamorous and sexy, most people find others less attractive when they smoke, according to a study which involved college students. Eddie Clark, an assistant professor of psychology at Memphis State University in Tennessee who conducted the study, said "the basic finding was that despite what advertisements would have us believe, both smokers and non-smokers tend to rate smokers less attractive. . . . Cigarette ads portray people who smoke as glamorous and sexy, but that's not what the real image of a smoker is, the "Gender and Smoking Status" report concluded.

Clark and his colleagues asked 229 college students to watch videotapes of male and female models as smokers or nonsmokers and then asked them to rate their attractiveness and state their impressions about the models' sexual appeal. The next report shows that the nonsmokers were rated more highly on an attractiveness scale, even by the viewers who smoked themselves. While both male and female smokers were rated as less attractive, smoking appeared to diminish women's attractiveness the most. Clark summarized, "If you compare smoking women to non-smoking women and smoking men to non-smoking men, in both cases chances are the smoker is the one that is going to be liked less. That effect is much stronger for women than men."

Analysis of the research showed the male nonsmokers rated an average of fifty-two on an attractiveness scale compared to forty-two for smokers. Female nonsmokers rated an average of sixty-eight compared to forty-seven for smokers. Twelve would be the worst rating, 108 would be the best rating.

The report said smokers were rated higher on a scale measuring the viewers' impressions of their sexual activity. On a scale of one to seven, the average rating for the smokers on the videotape was four compared to three for nonsmokers. "What this is probably saying is they are being perceived as promiscuous. It's sexual activity of a negative sort," said Clark. Despite decades of cigarette advertising, male subjects also indicated a greater preference for engaging in intimate behavior with female nonsmokers than female smokers. Clark said that all findings held true regardless of whether the viewers were smokers. "You would think that smokers would not have that bias, that they would not see that person as less likeable or more promiscuous. But that's not true," according to Clark and his colleagues, who cite a number of interesting sources in their study on the "glamorous" side of smoking.[2] Most of these research studies contradict or repudiate the image portrayed in most tobacco advertising.

Typical of the smooth and attractive image in tobacco advertising is the magazine *Philip Morris: The Best of America,* published quarterly by Philip Morris USA (New York). It is a sophisticated, glossy, trendy magazine. The June 1988 issue features an attractive canoeist on the cover and has perhaps a dozen pages of colored photographs of bronzed, athletic youth and adults jogging, canoeing, and so on. Those featured often have cigarettes in hand. A popular feature is always the "letters to the editor" section—in this issue are smokers' complaints about in-flight smoking bans, pending indoor clean air legislation, and restrictions on their freedom of choice. The feature in the June 1988 issue (volume 3: 21-29) was a reader survey conducted by Roper's—the more than 400,000 respondents were "better educated, more politically and socially active, and have higher family incomes than do American adults in general." The magazine stressed that PM's readers represent a $1 trillion market with tens of millions of smokers—"too much financial power to ignore." This carefuly cultivated image of typical smokers is exactly the picture the magazine wishes to project. PM's readers are "movers and shakers" (p. 23).

Not too many years ago some cigarette ads featured what appeared to be "medical doctors" in their ads. Advertisements were carefully worded to suggest the product(s) were "safe" and "healthy" and the "MDs" in the ads were obviously smoking. Contrast that approach with the present medical response. The U.S. surgeon general, C. Everett Koop, has called for a "total package of motivation, education, and training efforts" to achieve a "smokeless society by 2000." Koop suggests greater than 90 percent of physicians are nonsmokers and urges physicians do more than just admonish the patients they see to quit—he wants active intervention by physicians and other health care providers to[3]

1. Provide information to their patients clarifying the risks associated with smoking.
2. Clarify the reduction of risk that will occur when their patients stop smoking.
3. Encourage abstinence with advice and direct service.
4. Refer patients to smoking cessation programs.
5. Provide specific cessation and maintenance strategies from doctors' offices.

Industrial hygienists, among others, have joined in this call for activism—the chairperson of the American Industrial Hygiene Association's occupational medicine committee said "Hygienists have the right, and obligation, to help in the fight to restrict employees' smoking on the job." See "Hygienists Set Sights on Smoke-free Workplace," *National Safety and Health News* 134 (August 1986): 58-61.

A physician at the University of Utah, John H. Holbrook, helped compile the 1985 surgeon general's report on smoking. Holbrook has reported that "passive smokers" (those who breathe the smoke expelled into the air by smokers) have the following problems:[4]

• Children reared in homes with smoking parents are more likely to be hospitalized with pneumonia or bronchitis in their first year of life. The lungs of infants exposed to tobacco smoke don't mature normally.

• In adults, there is universal acknowledgment of the irritation factor associated with sidestream smoke—tearing of the eyes, tickling of the throat, headaches, and other effects.

• At the workplace, workers exposed to sidestream smoke forty hours a week have effects similar to smoking several cigarettes a day.

• Nonsmokers can experience a measurable decline in lung function when exposed to others' smoke.

• Although an increased incidence of lung cancer in passive smokers has not been indisputably established, thirteen of fifteen studies indicated a positive correlation for increased risk for the spouses of smokers.

• Patients with established heart or lung problems may experience symptoms sooner in a smoke-filled atmostphere than they otherwise would. For instance, smoke will trigger pain in people who have angina pectoris (heart pain related to partially blocked blood vessels). Those who have pulmonary problems will experience shortness of breath or cough sooner.

- There appears to be a correlation in deaths from heart attack among those exposed to sidestream smoke, compared to those who are not. The findings are preliminary, says Holbrook, and more study is needed to substantiate the indications.

Again, we should note that the Tobacco Institute is critical of most of this research (see Chapter 2).

As addressed in greater detail in Chapters 6 and 7, smoking in the workplace is no longer a policy that can be treated lightly. Typical is one comment in a personnel journal that "the wise company is one that responds quickly and seriously to complaints concerning smoking in the work place—just as it would to complaints about sexual or other prohibited harassment."[5] Smoking on the job is now a key issue and one that demands an affirmative response (see Chapter 8 for suggested policies and next steps for implementing a nonsmoking program at the workplace). Not just the U.S. Army or corporate executives or college students' attractiveness to one another or MDs, including the U.S. surgeon general, or even passive smokers, but "wise companies" are now concerned with employees who use tobacco. The 1985 surgeon general's report summarized the following discrete findings for workers in hazardous environments:[6]

- The highest smoking rate for men, 55.1 percent, was found among painters, construction workers, and maintenance workers. Often, therefore, workers who are already "at risk" are the heaviest smokers.
- Slightly more than 53 percent of all truck drivers smoke, compared to 53 percent of construction laborers, 50.8 percent of carpenters and auto mechanics, and 50.5 percent of guards and watchmen.
- The lowest rates of smoking for men occurred among electrical and electronic engineers, 16.2 percent. Others with low smoking rates were lawyers, 21.9 percent; secondary school teachers, 24.9 percent; accountants, 26.8 percent; real estate agents, 27.8 percent; and farmers, 28.1 percent.
- The disparity in smoking rates by occupation was less for women than for men.
- Waitresses smoked the most at 51.1 percent, wile 44.2 percent of cashiers, 42.9 percent of assembly line workers and 41 percent of nurse aides and orderlies were smokers.

Later chapters of this book show what private companies and government agencies are doing about smoking when workers are in hazardous occupations—including total bans on the use of tobacco products by employees on and *off* the job. While these cases are statistically few, they may represent a growing trend. For instance, the *Kansas City Star* (November 17, 1985: 12A) reported:

New police officers in Holden, Massachusetts will not be allowed to smoke—not in the police station, not in a cruiser, not on the street and not even in the privacy of their homes.

A new contract with the town's police officers provides that officers hired after September 5 must be non-smokers and that those hired as non-smokers can be disciplined or dismissed if they start to smoke. Town officials and the union said they thought it was the first such contract in the nation.

Current employees are excluded, but the last two smokers among the 17 full-time police officers in Holden, a suburb of 14,000 people seven miles northwest of Worcester in central Massachusetts, quit smoking earlier this year.

The contract was approved in August by a vote of 16 to 1 and the dissenter voted against it for reasons unrelated to the ban on smoking.

A telephone interview (July 6, 1988) with the Holden chief of police indicates the program/ban has been "extra successful" and is working well. In fact, the city has coupled the ban with a $500 bonus each year for demonstrated physical fitness.

Cartoons and cigars, pipes, and cigarettes seem to naturally go together. A minute's reflection can typically bring to recall various cartoon characters who smoke or puff or chew. Yet this, too, has gone through some societal change of late. Just one example, for instance is that of T. Casey Brennan, a former writer of comic book scripts. He set out to de-glamorize smoking "by taking it out of the hands of the 'good guys.' " He feels progress has been slow but steady—some of the biggest cartoon heroes no longer smoke, but too many cartoon characters still are identified with tobacco. Brennan worries that impressionable young readers are likely to "identify with" cartoon characters dependent on tobacco.[7]

Virtually anyone who has ever flown on a domestic or international flight knows the issue of smoking versus nonsmoking from a firsthand point of view. Smokers feel their rights have been trampled on—squashed into the back rows of the plane; nonsmokers, however, complain about passive smoke. Even flight attendants feel their health is endangered by poor cabin air quality. Each year Americans fly on more than 300 million plane trips; these flights are served by some 70,000 flight attendants. A careful analysis of the health and safety of these persons—cabin air quality, medical statistics on air travel, recommendations on smoking bans on domestic flights—has been reported on by the National Research Council. The recent smoking ban by the U.S. Department of Transportation on short flights doesn't seem to have satisfied anyone in particular.[8]

Thus, in perhaps two generations smoking has lost much of its glamour and appeal in this country and abroad. Despite efforts by the Tobacco Institute to rebut medical research, despite dozens of successful defenses of the tobacco industry before judges and juries, and despite the Tobacco Institute's carefully modulated appeal to reason, accommodation, and compromise, smoking has lost favor in the eyes of most Americans. Fewer Americans smoke,[9] the habit has become less attractive in various ways, the U.S. government officially seeks a smokeless society, and even the Tobacco Institute and the tobacco industry have drawn negative press from the advertising industry itself (where tobacco firms have spent millions of dollars over decades) for tobacco's heavy-handed tactics.[10]

Lastly, as *Newsweek* put it, "You wouldn't think there was much bad left to be said about smoking in the United States." Then in 1988 Surgeon General Koop charged nicotine "is every bit as addicting as those headline grabbing substances of abuse, heroin and cocaine." And the debate starts over again.[11] American society has made a very wide swing from tobacco and smoking being the featured habit of movie stars and top athletes to where even the U.S. Army goes smokeless and calls it "the end of an era." All kinds of health insurers and providers now promote nonsmoking. It is not just a fad but an issue of quality of life and healthcare cost containment.[12]

The Tobacco Institute, a trade association of U.S. cigarette manufacturers, has said:[13]

Where safety such as in a chemistry lab is not an issue, individual companies should be free to work out smoking policies short of a draconian ban on smoking. The institute opposes smoking legislation and believes that smoking is an adult decision. We don't encourage smoking or quitting. It's a matter of choice.

Robert D. Tollison is a George Mason University professor who has done research on behalf of the Tobacco Institute. Tollison disputes research findings of the anti-smoking lobby.[14] He says that smoking restrictions actually cost companies about $900 annually per smoking employee because of lost time spent in smoking lounges or other restricted areas. The Tobacco Institute claims that no scientific studies, including the surgeon general's report, prove a link between passive smoke and nonsmokers' health problems. "It's a pretty poor idea to base a policy on science that won't support it," says Walker C. Merryman, Tobacco Institute vice president.[15] Still, societal changes seem to mitigate against the tobacco industry. Times have changed: The mood is nonsmoking on the job and, sometimes, off the job.

The courts have not been unanimous in deciding cases concerning smokers' versus nonsmokers' rights. Still, the following cases can be cited as examples of societal (judicial) change.

- The U.S. Supreme Court upheld a total ban on cigarettes in *Austin* vs. *Tennessee,* 179 U.S. 343 (1900), if the ban "is designed for the protection of the public health."
- The U.S. 9th Circuit Court of Appeals (San Francisco) in *Parodi* vs. *Merit Systems Protection Board,* 690 F. 2d 731 (1982) ordered an employer to furnish a smokefree environment or pay disability payments until a worker reached retirement age (plus retroactive disability pay).
- The Missouri Court of Appeals held in *Smith* vs. *Western Electric,* 643 SW 2d 10 (1982) that an employee had the right to a totally smokefree work environment.
- A federal court in Seattle in *Vickers* vs. *Veteran's Administration, et al.,* 549 F Supp. 85 (1982) ruled an employee had the right to be free of "passive" or secondhand smoke.
- The Washington Supreme Court ruled in *McCarthy* vs. *The Department of Social and Health Services,* No. 53548-5 (1988), the employer must take reasonable steps to accommodate an employee sensitive to passive smoke.
- The most cited case is *Donna Shimp* vs. *New Jersey Bell Telephone Company,* 368 A 2d 408 (1976) in New Jersey, where the court ordered a nonsmoking environment.

There are numerous labor relations cases before administrative law judges, arbitrators, Equal Employment Opportunity Commission decisions, National Labor Relations Board decisions, Occupational Safety Health Administration decisions, and others that turn on the same issue. The Tobacco Institute argues cases like Shimp "are a legal fluke."[16] Obviously, cases can be cited that did not uphold smokers' rights. In general courts seem to be moving in the direction of the surgeon general's smokeless society.

NOTES

1. The full study is titled "Attributions about Sexual Behavior and Attractiveness as a Function of Subjects' and Targets' Gender and Smoking Status." The research was supported by a grant from the National Heart, Lung, and Blood Institute and a grant from the State of Tennessee.

2. Ibid; some of these citations are on pages 12-13 of the "Gender and Smoking Status" survey, as follows: Barton, J., Chassin L., Presson, C. C., and Sherman, S. J., "Social Image Factors as Motivators of Smoking Initiation in Early and Middle Adolescence," *Child Development* 53 (1982): 1499-1511. Carll, E. K., "Perception of the Personal Attributes of Male and Female Smokers as a Function of Sex and

Smoking Status of the Observer," *Dissertation Abstracts International* 38 (1978): 5641-B (University Microfilms No. 78-06162). Charlton, A., "Smoking and Weight Control in Teenagers," *Public Health London* 98 (1984): 277-81. Delaney, J. W., "Perception of Adult Smokers by Schoolchildren," *Dissertation Abstracts International* 39 (1978): 1539-B (University Microfilms No. 78-14971). Germer, P., and Miller, R. E., "How Peers Perceive the Female Adult Smoker," *Journal of School Health* 54 (1984): 285-87. McKennell, A. C., and Bynner, J. M., "Self-Images and Smoking Behavior among School Boys," *British Journal of Education* 39 (1969): 27-39. Noppa, H., and Bengtsson, C., "Obesity in Relation to Smoking: A Population Study of Women in Göteborg, Sweden," *Preventive Medicine* 9 (1980): 534-43. Polivy, J., Hackett, R., and Bycio, P., "The Effect of Perceived Smoking Status on Attractiveness," *Personality and Social Psychology Bulletin* 5 (1979): 401-4. Weir, J. M., "Male Student Perceptions of Smokers," in S. V. Zagona, ed., *Studies and Issues in Smoking Behavior* Tucson: University of Arizona Press, 1967): 151-55.

3. Koop, "Is a Smokeless Society by 2000 Achievable?" *Archives of Internal Medicine* 145 (September 1985): 1581.

4. "A Dark, Ominous Cloud of Evidence Hovers over 'Passive Smoker,' " *Deseret News* (January 18, 1986): 18A.

5. James R. Williams, "A Smoldering Issue: Cigarettes at Work," *Personnel* 62 (July 1985): 17-20.

6. "Workplace Can Pose High Risk to Smokers," *Deseret News* (December 19, 1985): A1.

7. Peter Ozorio, "Cartoon Heroes Needn't Smoke!" *World Health* (January-February 1986): 9.

8. For example, see "Bills to Snuff In-Flight Smoking Backed," *American Medical News* (October 23, 1987): 2; "Plane Smoking Sparks Capital Debate," *Travel Weekly* 46 (October 15, 1987); Gabriel Phillips, "ATA: Smoke Ban Singles Out Aviation," *Travel Weekly* 45 (October 2, 1986): 102; "New York Justice Upholds Smoking Ban on Trains," *Wall Street Journal* (March 8, 1988): National Research Council, *The Airliner Cabin Environment: Air Quality and Safety* (Washington, D.C.: National Academy Press, 1986).

9. "Regional Variation in Smoking Prevalence and Cessation," *Journal of the American Medical Association* 258 (December 18, 1987): 3368.

10. See "Truth the Casualty in PM's War," *Advertising Age* 58 (October 12, 1987): 16.

11. "Getting Hooked on Tobacco," *Newsweek* 111 (May 30, 1988): 56.

12. As but one example, see CIGNA Healthplans of California, *Time to Quit: Smoking Kit* (Glendale: CIGNA, 1986). See also materials quoted in Chapter 8 of this text.

13. Marc Reisch, "Smoking Restrictions Multiply in Chemical Company Offices," *Chemical and Engineering News* 66 (March 18, 1987): 16.

14. See the Tobacco Institute's rigorous rebuttal of "Research Evidence on Environmental Tobacco Smoke," in Robert D. Tollison, ed., *Clearing the Air* (Lexington, Mass.: Lexington Books, 1988): 119-44.

15. See the discussion of these cases in "Smoking Bans Are Legal!" in William L. Weis and Bruce W. Miller, *The Smokefree Workplace* (Buffalo: Prometheus Books, 1985): 71-80. A vigorous rebuttal of the position can be found in "Smoking, Human Rights, and Civil Liberties," in Robert D. Tollison, ed., *Smoking and Society: Toward a More Balanced Assessment* (Lexington, Mass.: Lexington Books, 1986): 189-213.

16. See "Legal Developments," in Bureau of National Affairs, *Where There's Smoke: Problems and Policies Concerning Smoking in the Workplace* (Rockville, Md.: Bureau of National Affairs, 1986): 31-43, esp. 32.

5

THE PUBLIC HEALTH ISSUE

In earlier chapters of this book we have tried to document the scope of the smoking controversy, the costs of smoking, changes in societal values and attitudes, and the history of the surgeon general's reports to Congress on smoking. We will not duplicate all of these data here. The American Cancer Society in a 1985 pamphlet called "Model Policy for Smoking in the Workplace" summarized some facts about cigarette smoking and smokers:

FACT: Smoking is a major cause of heart disease.

Smokers have twice the risk of dying of heart attacks.

Smokers die of strokes three times as often as nonsmokers.

Smokers who are over 35 and use oral contraceptives are in a high risk group for heart attack and stroke.

FACT: Smoking is the cause of about 30 percent of all cancers.

Smoking is responsible for more than 83 percent of lung cancer cases overall.

Smoking increases risk of the disease tenfold.

Smoking will soon make lung cancer the number one cancer killer of American women.

FACT: Smoking is specifically related to 80 percent of emphysema and 75 percent of chronic bronchitis.

FACT: Smoking increases the risk of miscarriage, lowers birth weight, raises a baby's chances of complications at delivery and the likelihood of health problems during infancy.

FACT: Smoking-related disorders are estimated to cause about 350,000 premature deaths each year.

FACT: Smoking is responsible for lost work days.

Smokers have a 33 to 45 percent excess absenteeism rate as compared to nonsmokers.

These kinds of data are more thoroughly presented elsewhere in this book, along with the Tobacco Institute's rebuttals. Still, the incumbent surgeon general of the United States made the following conclusions in his 1986 report to Congress:

1. Involuntary smoking (secondhand or passive smoke) is a cause of disease, including lung cancer in healthy nonsmokers.
2. The children of parents who smoke compared with the children of nonsmoking parents have an increased frequency of respiratory infections, increased respiratory symptoms, and slightly smaller rates of increase in lung function as the lung matures.
3. The simple separation of smokers and nonsmokers within the same air space may reduce, but does not eliminate, the exposure of nonsmokers to environmental tobacco smoke.

Dr. Koop in 1988 also called tobacco an "addictive substance" (see below).

The National Research Council in *Environmental Tobacco Smoke: Measuring Exposures and Assessing Health Effects* stated that much of the concern today about smoking is the impact of passive or secondhand smoke on nonsmokers. Persons exposed to secondhand smoke are actually at greater risk in an undiluted atmosphere than the smoker. Tobacco smoke contains more than 3,800 compounds; about 300 to 400 have been measured under standard laboratory smoking conditions, in both smoke collected directly from the end of a cigarette and sidestream smoke. Undiluted secondhand smoke contains some toxic compounds in much higher concentrations than mainstream smoke.

State chapters of the American Lung Association exist in all fifty states. ALA has had considerable success in designing and conducting smoking cessation programs. ALA has completed many studies on smoking cessation and the conclusion was that no one program is universally successful. That is, what works for one person may not help another.[1] ALA's seven programs are based on a lifestyle change and they have been professionally developed by teams of scientists, behaviorists, and educators on the basis of what ALA has learned about the smoking cessation process.[2] For people to be successful they must find out some basic things about their lifestyle and smoking habits: (1)

how and why they smoke, (2) what triggers them to smoke, (3) how to cope with their smoking habit, and finally (4) how they can design their own individualized program. ALA programs are designed so that each person using these four steps can write their own program and therefore be successful in becoming a nonsmoker. ALA programs are divided into two basic methods. This approach is strongly supported by extensive community research and experiences of others with helping smokers to quit.[3]

ALA'S SELF-HELP PROGRAMS

Freedom from Smoking in Twenty Days

A self-help program using a programmed learning manual and a maintenance manual. It is an intelligent, step-by-step, day-by-day program designed to help a person become a nonsmoker. No classes, no meetings, just a simple do-it-yourself program complete with work materials. Many corporations and the U.S. armed forces use this module. The module requires a daily thirty-minute effort for twenty consecutive days. The program is highly structured.

Freedom from Smoking for You and Your Family

A self-help manual written in a magazine format. A proven program for the person who wants the up-to-date cessation methods and is ready to quit today. Includes the latest material on nicotine gum and the latest facts on gradual reduction of the need for nicotine. A smoking cessation program and "stay quit" materials are combined in one book—easy and to the point.

Freedom from Smoking for You and Your Baby

A self-help manual produced in cooperation with the American Lung Association and Harvard Community Health Plan. Combines the cessation and maintenance program into one book. This program is tailored to the pregnant woman and is written with an understanding of both smoking addiction and the pressures of pregnancy. The cessation and maintenance program also includes an exercise and relaxation tape.

ALA's CLINICS

Double Plus Program

This modification of ALA's self-help method provides for a group of individuals (employees, club, neighborhood) to organize for a group effort to quit. Preparation, clarification, motivation, and buddy system are added through two group meetings (on successive days or every other day intervals) before the people go through their own individual quit-and-maintenance process linked to one or more partners with the self-help module.

Hypnosis Cessation Clinics

This is a group hypnosis program in one two-hour session. In addition to instruction, the individuals go through hypnosis three times. A cassette tape is given so that individuals can do a self-hypnosis follow-up and maintenance on succeeding days with the voice of the hypnotherapist. Hypnosis clinics are conducted three or four times a year. The program is suitable for individuals in publicly scheduled clinics or for employee groups, usually during daytime hours. Employers may call ALA to arrange for on-site clinics. These require a room for the group hypnosis and a minimum of twenty prepaid and preregistered employees or spouses. Special company sessions can be arranged.

Freedom from Smoking Clinic

This is an intense, hand-holding group process program that carries the person through eight sessions in eight weeks at irregular intervals (not weekly sessions). It is unique in that the smoker quits at the beginning of the program and then goes through a highly structured activity process for seven weeks to stay stopped. Thus, it has the highest success rate of any other ALA program. ALA's Freedom from Smoking Clinic requires highly trained and skilled personnel to conduct the clinic properly. Therefore, it is typically franchised by the American Lung Association to area hospitals to conduct. The ALA can schedule a special in-house Freedom from Smoking Clinic for corporations or government agencies.

In Control

This is ALA's home video module that permits the smoker to go through a simulated Freedom from Smoking Clinic. The module contains all a smoker needs to quit: a two-hour video cassette (thirteen nine-minute daily segments), 124-page viewer's workbook, and an audio cassette for relaxation. The use of nicotine gum is discussed. Employers and other groups or organizations may purchase one or more modules for loan or rental to their employees or members. Thus, the video tape can be used over and over. The workbook and audio cassette are expendable and have to be replaced through quantity purchase from the American Lung Association. For companies purchasing multiple copies (three or more), ALA offers a discount.

These self-help and clinical programs of the American Lung Association have been very successful and have helped many thousands of smokers to quit permanently. ALA has stated the following changes a person's body goes through when he or she quits smoking.[4]

Within twenty minutes of the last cigarette:
    Blood pressure drops to normal
    Pulse rate drops to normal rate
    Body temperature of hands and feet increase to normal

Within eight hours of the last cigarette:
    Carbon monoxide level in blood drops to normal
    Oxygen level in blood increases to normal

Twenty-four hours:
    Chance of heart attack decreases

Forty-eight hours:
    Nerve endings start regrowing
    Ability to smell and to taste things is enhanced

Seventy-two hours:
    Bronchial tubes relax, making breathing easier
    Lung capacity increases

Two weeks to three months:
    Circulation improves
    Lung function increases up to 30 percent
    Walking becomes easier

One to nine months:
    Coughing, sinus congestion, fatigue, and shortness of breath decrease
    Body's overall energy level increases
    Cilia regrow in lungs, increasing ability to handle mucus, clean the lungs, and reduce infection

The American Heart Association has published a number of guides on nonsmoking. One of the most useful is "Weight Control Guidance in Smoking Cessation" (1987). Since weight gain is not inevitable, but common when people stop smoking, the AHA addresses four major problems:

1. Lengthened mealtimes—smokers previously hurried through dinner and then lit a cigarette. Now the ex-smoker finishes ahead of others and consumes second helpings; replaces after-dinner cigarette with rich desserts.

2. Oral craving. Has frequent desire for something in the mouth. Results in frequent nibbling, usually sweets. May often be a desire for something to hold in place of a cigarette.

3. Evening snack—munching when relaxed now replaces the cigarette.

4. Activities or certain social situations that lead to eating or drinking and a cigarette. Coffee breaks, cocktail parties, sporting events, and other smoking-associated situations may lead to overeating to avoid cigarettes.

The American Heart Association suggests a number of solutions to these common problems but acknowledges

Not all of these ideas will be appropriate for any one individual. However, an awareness that eating is an established pattern that can be altered through a number of techniques may awaken patients to evaluate their habits, define their problems and plan their own effective measures or techniques.

The American Cancer Society has widely publicized a "Quitter's Guide: 7 Day Plan to Help You Stop Smoking Cigarettes" (1978). ACS lists the benefits of quitting and briefly identifies why people smoke, then suggests seven steps to quit—basically a series of self-motivational steps and practical actions—including announcing "to your friends about your quit smoking project." ACS says "A public declaration makes your commitment all the more definite." ACS urges smokers who want to quit to switch to undesirable brands, to sniff jars of damp cigarette butts, to throw away matches and lighters (makes it harder to get a light if one falters), to exercise daily, and so forth. Of course, as Mark Twain once said "It's easy to quit smoking. I've done it a thousand times." So ACS suggests some practical "quit tips to help you stay quit." While ACS's "Quitter's Guide" doesn't go as far as the American Lung Association's "Smoking Cessation Programs," it is practical and can help (it has been used by many businesses). ACS does offer support group help called "FreshStart." They describe their process as follows:

FreshStart emphasizes that stopping smoking is a two-part process: (1) stopping and (2) staying stopped. Individuals differ as to which part is the most difficult for them. And so FreshStart deals with both processes: the group helps you to stop smoking as quickly as possible and to focus your energy on planning ahead to avoid going back to smoking.

The four group meetings you attend as part of the Cancer Society's FreshStart will be conducted as work sessions.

The National Cancer Institute, Bethesda, Maryland, published a small booklet in 1987 called "Clearing the Air: How to Quit Smoking and Quit for

Keeps" (44 pages). It describes ways for smokers to prepare themselves for quitting, warns the smoker what to expect (withdrawal), urges a buddy or support group, and suggests "ways of quitting": switching brands, cutting down the number of cigarettes smoked, changing behavior so the ex-smoker doesn't smoke "automatically" (after meals and so on), making smoking inconvenient, making smoking unpleasant, and so forth. The Institute recognizes ways of "quitting for keeps," knowing relapses are to be expected.

The Public Health Service of the U.S. Department of Health and Human Services put out two brochures (July 1985) "Quit It" and "For Good" covering many of the same steps and procedures as the American Lung Association, American Cancer Society, and others. However, they include "snack calories" to help prevent gaining weight as snacks replace smokes—a set of tables of calories for typical snacks.

The Public Health Service in 1984 published a "Self Test for Smokers." There were three short tests. The first test asks, "Do you want to change your smoking habits?" It lists twelve questions, as follows, and "How to Score."

		Strongly agree	Mildly agree	Mildly disagree	Strongly disagree
A.	Cigarette smoking might give me a serious illness.	4	3	2	1
B.	My cigarette smoking sets a bad example for others.	4	3	2	1
C.	I find cigarette smoking to be a messy kind of habit.	4	3	2	1
D.	Controlling my cigarette smoking is a challenge to me.	4	3	2	1
E.	Smoking causes shortness of breath.	4	3	2	1

		Strongly agree	Mildly agree	Mildly disagree	Strongly disagree
F.	If I quit smoking cigarettes it might influence others to stop.	4	3	2	1
G.	Cigarettes cause damage to clothing and other personal property.	4	3	2	1
H.	Quitting smoking would show that I have willpower.	4	3	2	1
I.	My cigarette smoking will have a harmful effect on my health.	4	3	2	1
J.	My Cigarette smoking influences others close to me to take up or continue smoking.	4	3	2	1
K.	If I quit smoking, my sense of taste or smell would improve.	4	3	2	1
L.	I do not like the idea of feeling dependent on smoking.	4	3	2	1

The authors will not reproduce here all the interpretative data and categories provided by the Public Health Service on "What Your Score Means" but the following statement from the Health Service suggests the importance of a smoker's score:

Test 1 of the Smoker's Self Test was designed to measure the importance of each of these reasons to you. The higher you score on any category, say health, the more important that reason is to you. A score of 9 or above in one of these categories indicates that this is one of the most important reasons why you may want to quit.

Test 2 of the Public Health Service's 1984 packet covers the effects of smoking. Test 3 poses the question "Why do you smoke?" and gives information on scoring, as follows:

		Always	Fre-quently	Occa-sionally	Seldom	Never
A.	I smoke cigarettes to keep myself from slowing down.	5	4	3	2	1
B.	Handling a cigarette is part of the enjoyment of smoking it.	5	4	3	2	1
C.	Smoking cigarettes is pleasant and relaxing.	5	4	3	2	1
D.	I light up a cigarette when I feel angry about something.	5	4	3	2	1
E.	When I have run out of cigarettes I find it almost unbearable until I can get them.	5	4	3	2	1

	Always	Fre-quently	Occa-sionally	Seldom	Never
F. I smoke cigarettes automatically without even being aware of it.	5	4	3	2	1
G. I smoke cigarettes to stimulate me, to perk myself up.	5	4	3	2	1
H. Part of the enjoyment of smoking a cigarette comes from the steps I take to light up.	5	4	3	2	1
I. I find cigarettes pleasurable.	5	4	3	2	1
J. When I feel uncomfortable or upset about something, I light up a cigarette.	5	4	3	2	1
K. I am very much aware of the fact when I am not smoking a cigarette.	5	4	3	2	1
L. I light up a cigarette without realizing I still have one burning in the ashtray.	5	4	3	2	1
M. I smoke cigarettes to give me a "lift."	5	4	3	2	1

44

		Always	Fre-quently	Occa-sionally	Seldom	Never
N.	When I smoke a cigarette, part of the enjoyment is watching the smoke as I exhale it.	5	4	3	2	1
O.	I want a cigarette most when I am comfortable and relaxed.	5	4	3	2	1
P.	When I feel "blue" or want to take my mind off cares and worries, I smoke cigarettes.	5	4	3	2	1
Q.	I get a real gnawing hunger for a cigarette when I haven't smoked for a while.	5	4	3	2	1
R.	I've found a cigarette in my mouth and didn't remember putting it there.	5	4	3	2	1

How to Score:

1. Write the number you have circled after each statement in Test 3 in the corresponding space to the right.

2. Add the scores down each column to get your totals. For example, the sum of your scores A, G, M gives you your score for the first column.

A ____	B ____	C ____	D ____	E ____	F ____
G ____	H ____	I ____	J ____	K ____	L ____
M ____	N ____	O ____	P ____	Q ____	R ____
Totals 1 ____	2 ____	3 ____	4 ____	5 ____	6 ____
Stimu-lation	Hand-ling	Pleas-ure	Crutch	Crav-ing	Habit

The Public Health Service interprets "What Your Score Means" on Test 3 in this way:

In this test examining reasons why you smoke, a score of 11 or above on any factor indicates that it is an important source of satisfaction for you. The higher you score (15 is the highest), the more important a particular factor is in your smoking and the more useful the discussion of that factor can be in your attempt to quit.

If you do not score high on any of the six factors, chances are that you do not smoke very much or have not been smoking for very many years. If so, giving up smoking—and staying off—should be easy.

The Public Health Service has seen wide distribution of its "Self Test for Smokers" booklet. The instrument can be very useful in preassessment of persons and groups before a company or agency smoking cessation program is initiated (along with other steps listed in Chapter 8).

These tests help to demonstrate one thing referred to in other chapters of this book—"light" smokers and newer smokers find it easier to succeed when an organization tries to implement smoking cessation programs. Hard-core smokers, particularly those who have smoked since their teens, are going to find it very hard to stop. If they succeed at all it will take intense motivation and possibly many attempts. Organizations must be prepared to make long-term assistance available.

The American Lung Association in their clinics quote a number of "Myths and Facts Regarding Smoking Cessation" as follows (from L. Schiffman, et al., in "Preventing Relapse in Ex-Smokers"):

Myth	Fact
Quitting is either easy or it is impossibly difficult.	Some people have very few withdrawal symptoms and find quitting to be fairly easy. Others may experience withdrawal symptoms or intense cravings that make quitting more difficult.
Quitting does not take any extra effort or time.	It is usually helpful to allocate extra time and energy to quitting.
Cravings for cigarettes last forever.	Individual cravings are typically short and decrease in frequency, while the intensity may not change.
If the initial quitting is hard, maintaining abstinence is equally difficult.	Quitting and maintaining abstinence are different and may require different strategies.
If you have any difficulty, it probably means you cannot quit or did not really want to. You might as well smoke.	Most people can expect some difficulty in quitting.
Feeling proud or successful after getting through a difficult time is a waste of time. After all, the battle is not over yet.	It is important to recognize and reinforce progress rather than interpret crises as signs of failure.
There is not much to know about quitting—it just takes wanting to.	There are definite coping skills and strategies that can be learned to manage quitting.
If you have had a hard time quitting in the past you can expect it to be hard in future quitting attempts.	Successive attempts at quitting are not necessarily the same. In fact, previous quits may provide insights and skill development for future quits.
It does not make any difference when you try to quit, or, it is best to wait for the "perfect quit date."	Timing may be an important consideration that may affect a client's success in quitting.

Resource, published by the American Society for Personnel Administration, reported in June 1988 (7:14): "A report released by the federal government proposing that cigarette smoking be officially declared an addiction and that smokers be treated as disability victims could have a profound impact upon American businesses." *Resource* went on to say that Surgeon General C. Everett Koop's 618-page report declared that research "firmly supports the premise that nicotine in tobacco products is an addictive drug comparable to heroin or morphine." Koop also said that "smokers should be treated as having a disability, similar to those being treated for alcoholism." The surgeon general's report said "cigarette smoking is responsible for more than 300,000 deaths in the United States each year—more than twice the number of alcohol-related deaths, 75 times as many as heroin, 150 times the number caused by cocaine."

Resource reported that, currently, forty-two states have laws prohibiting the practice of discrimination against the hiring of handicapped persons. The personnel newsletter added, however, should smoking be declared a handicap, in light of the status of other addictions in many jurisdictions, the declaration would run counter to recent trends toward smoking restrictions and smoke-free workplaces. *Resource* was concerned that, "for businesses, treating cigarette smokers as disabled persons could affect a company's bottom line—through costs of rehabilitation programs, leaves from the office and possibly discrimination suits." The publication commented, "It's conceivable that those businesses that have a smoke-free policy could face being sued because to deny a smoker his right to light up is to discriminate against a handicapped person, if you carry his [Koop's] remarks to the limit." The surgeon general's report also "called upon insurers to pay for treatment programs to help smokers quit, as they do for treatment programs for alcoholics and those addicted to other drugs," quoted *Resource*.

The tobacco industry, as represented by their trade association, the Tobacco Institute, rejects, however, Koop's analysis and says that smoking is a personal choice by individuals, "a choice any smoker can willingly give up at any time." *Resource* quotes the Tobacco Institute as saying that "the surgeon general's report trivializes the serious drug problem faced by society. The claims that smokers are 'addicts' defy common sense and contradict the fact that people quit smoking every day." Walker Merryman, a spokesman for the Tobacco Institute, cited as an example the 40 million smokers who have given up "the habit." And 95 percent of those 40 million gave up smoking of their own volition, Merryman told *Resource*. "It is fundamentally wrong to equate cigarette smoking to illegal drugs such as cocaine and heroin. It sends the wrong message to those who voluntarily wish to smoke, because cigarette smoking does not impair one's senses the way illegal drugs do." ASPA's *Resource* concluded by saying, "Anti-smoking activists said the report would help former smokers suing tobacco companies because they suffered damage to their health. No plaintiff has won such a case or received damages in a settlement." Lawyers for tobacco companies in such suits "depend almost entirely on portraying the smoker as having freedom of choice," said Matthew Myers, staff director of the Coalition on Smoking and Health.

Chapter 8 provides extensive examples of designing and installing nonsmoking programs. But where companies are considering putting smokers in the same category as other workers in employee assistance programs (EAPs), these additional resources may help:

William A. Carnahan, *Legal Issues Affecting Employee Assistance Programs* (Arlington, Va.: The Association of Labor-Management Administrators and Consultants on Alcoholism, 1984).

Donald W. Myers, *Employee Assistance Programs: Drug, Alcohol, and Other Problems* (Chicago: Commerce Clearing House, 1986).

Richard L. Hawks and C. Nora Chiang, eds., *Urine Testing for Drugs of Abuse* (Rockville, Md.: National Institute on Drug Abuse, 1986, Monograph 73).

J. Michael Walsh and Steven W. Gust, eds., *Interdisciplinary Approaches to the Problem of Drug Abuse in the Workplace* (Washington, D.C.: Public Health Service, DHHS Publication No. [ADM] 86-1477, 1986).

Arthur D. Rutkowski, "Feature: Comprehensive Substance Abuse Program, Policies, and Employment Assistance Program for Union and Non-union Employees," in *Employment Law Update* (Evansville, Ind.: Rutkowski and Associates, 1986).

Richard J. Coelho, *Quitting Smoking: A Psychological Experiment Using Community Research* (New York: Peter Lang, 1985).

Ruth A. Behrens, *A Decision Maker's Guide to Reducing Smoking At the Worksite* (Washington, D.C.: Washington Business Group on Health, 1985).

Dr. Koop summarized the public health issues from the government's perspective as follows:[5]

I first called for a "smoke-free society" by the year 2000 three years ago. What I meant was a society in which nobody would smoke tobacco in the presence of others without permission. I didn't know then if this smoke-free millennium could be achieved. Seeing what has happened in the past three years, I feel sure it can. . . .

Now, following my latest report and other growing evidence, the American Cancer Society, American Heart Association and American Lung Association are moving together against this public-health hazard. While they work independently at state and local levels for enactment of clean-indoor-air legislation, in 1982 they formed the Coalition on Smoking or Health to pursue legislation at the federal level.

How can we achieve a smoke-free society by the year 2000? It won't be easy, despite signs of progress. The non-smoking forces are up against a heavily financed, politically powerful tobacco industry.

NOTES

1. For instance, *Consumer Reports* for August 1984 (434-35) described early tests on Nicorette (a nicotine resin complex) approved in 1984 as a chewing gum by the Food and Drug Administration. It is a prescription drug intended as a "temporary aid for smokers trying to quit." *Consumer Reports* summarized field research trials: "First, bear in mind that the participants in the trials were all highly motivated to quit. If

you're not eager to give up smoking, *Nicorette* is unlikely to be of much help. Second, and more important, is that few smokers succeed in quitting permanently on the first try—or even on the first few attempts. It can take several efforts to achieve long-term success. If you've tried and failed before but still want to quit, *Nicorette* offers another opportunity. It's nothing like a sure-fire cure, but it is the first product to come along that just might increase your chances of succeeding."

2. See American Lung Association's "Smoking Cessation Programs" flyer, photocopied, and distributed by state chapters. This material has been edited herein but is largely intact.

3. See Richard J. Coelho, *Quitting Smoking: A Psychological Experiment Using Community Research* (New York: Peter Lang, 1985). Coelho's bibliography (284-95) includes 155 references.

4. ALA, "Smoking Cessation Programs."

5. C. Everett Koop, "Non-smokers: Time to Clear the Air," *Reader's Digest* (April 1987) reprint.

6

THE RESPONSE BY
GOVERNMENT AGENCIES

Government agencies at all levels have responded to the smoking on the job issue. The public sector response has been influenced, in part, by the nature of public services. An example of the response of government agencies (state and local) toward smoking on the job is in the job category of firefighter.

Firefighting is recognized as one of the most hazardous occupations in the United States. Indeed, many states treat most firefighter heart and respiratory disorders as a presumptive job-related disability and thus award disability retirement to injured workers. Obviously, heart, lung, or other respiratory disability is costly for the state or local fire department and insurers. A few fire systems in the country have, therefore, chosen to restrict smoking. Some restrict smoking on and off the job.

The City of Virginia Beach, Virginia, requires *all* uniformed employees in the fire department to sign a binding contract with the key clause being: "[*employee name*] agrees that upon employment, he/she will not smoke nor utilize smoking material considered as dangerous within the framework of controlled substance statutes on or off duty. This condition to be in effect during the entire tenure of the employee." The fire chief of Virginia Beach in a telephone interview with the authors (on February 19, 1986) stressed that this is a condition of employment only for new firefighters, but will be enforced (up to and including discharge for noncompliance). He noted that the city completed a survey recently where more than 80 percent of the firefighters identified themselves as nonsmokers and favored such a tough new policy. Obviously a double standard of compliance will exist where "old timers" will be allowed, under grandfather clauses, to smoke and new hires will not. The nonsmoking provision will uniformly apply to bunk areas, dining room, and other areas, but smoking will be permitted for old timers in general work areas of the stations. The fire chief admitted he has "drawn some bad press (along with much positive press commentary)" and has "been called a fascist dictator" by some detractors. Virginia does not have a public employee collective bargaining law, but the chief said his "recent employee survey showed more than three-fourths of the 80 percent supporting the nonsmoking policy were union members [International Association of Fire Fighters], so the new policy is not an issue with the union itself."

The city of Virginia Beach has had at least one "incident come up between smokers/non-smokers where management/supervisors had to intervene" and has "designed an office or structured an office layout at least in part because of the smoking/non-smoking issue in non-uniformed employee settings." The city segregates smokers and nonsmokers in work areas or stations "and in office/room assignments." The city "provides or makes available programs (counseling, therapy groups, other formal means of employee assistance) to help employees stop (or cut down on) smoking," and includes specific references on the issue in new employee orientation.[1]

The fire department of the village of Skokie, Illinois, also requires new hires to sign an agreement as below:

Fire Department
Condition of Employment Agreement

I,_____, acknowledge that by accepting employment with the Village of Skokie Fire Department as a Firefighter/Paramedic, I am agreeing to the following condition of employment: From my date of hire, I will not smoke, chew or use any tobacco product(s) on or off duty during the entire tenure of my employment; if I do smoke, chew or use any tobacco product(s) at any time during the entire tenure of my employment, I will be subject to dismissal for cause. I understand this condition; agree to it; and accept such a condition of employment with the Village of Skokie.

_____,   _____
           signature   date

A personnel officer for Oklahoma City, Oklahoma, wrote the authors, "This City's fire department has a nonsmoking policy for first year recruits. After one year they are free [again] to smoke. One recruit was terminated because of [violation of] this policy. He filed suit in our District Court. The judge dismissed the case. The employee then filed with the Equal Employment Opportunity Commission. They found no probable cause [for his charge of discrimination]."

Hampton Roads, Louisiana, has a nonsmoking policy for new fire and police (sworn) personnel, a policy recommended by its city attorney.

Typical of many smaller cities in the written policy of the city of Oakland Park, Florida (with 281 employees). Florida passed a Clean Indoor Air Act in 1985. This city provides for mediation of disputes between smokers and non-smokers by immediate supervisors but does not provide any elaborate detailing of procedures or means of enforcement. The city's policy reads in part:

In work areas, where space is shared by two or more persons, an effort shall be made to accommodate individual preferences to the degree prudently possible. When requested, supervisors shall make a reasonable attempt to mediate a settlement and/or separate persons who smoke from those who do not.

Employees may designate their private offices as smoking or non-smoking areas. Visitors to private work areas will honor the wishes of the host.

In City-owned vehicles, smoking shall be permitted only when there is no objection from one or more of the occupants. Employees and visitors are expected to honor the smoke and non-smoking designations and to be considerate of non-smokers in their vicinity.

Oakland Park attempts to resolve conflicts by courtesy, consideration, and good will, but still stipulates that when "accommodation is not possible, the rights of the non-smoker should prevail." Further response added that "majority rule" has been the policy to date and that "a vast majority are non-smokers." The city office building has only one small lunchroom (which seats perhaps twenty persons) and nonsmokers have not complained about smoking there because it is "recognized that the lunchroom is the only place smokers can go, because virtually every office area is off-limits now, unless there is a supervisor who smokes who will let an employee smoke in the supervisor's own office.'

The city of Salem, Oregon, has about 1,500 municipal employees. The city is covered under a state law on smoking, and implemented the following policy in 1983 (as revised several times since):

Smoking in City Facilities

General Discussion
The purpose of this letter is to establish a policy regarding smoking in city facilities which provides a smoke-free work environment for employees.

Policy
Smoking is prohibited in all city buildings, except as listed below. Smoking is also prohibited in city equipment where any occupant objects.
Smoking is permitted in:

- The City Hall restaurant, except where posted otherwise
- Engine bays of all Fire Stations
- Any completely enclosed room which can be designated by the Department Head to be used exclusively for smoking.

As noted earlier, industrial injury claims have become extremely costly for many communities in recent years, especially for firefighters. As a consequence, Salem's Civil Service Commission also amended its civil service rules in 1983 to prohibit smoking on or off the job by firefighters (because of city liability under Oregon's Occupational Disease Law) as follows: "Firefighters appointed after March 9, 1983 must not smoke tobacco either on or off duty during their term of employment."

Salem's firefighter rule naturally attracted considerable press coverage and controversy. The city's personnel director strongly endorsed the policy for firefighters on cost containment grounds alone. In a telephone interview on February 10, 1986 he told the authors that controversy has now largely died down and only two incidents have recently arisen—neither involving firefighters. Salem's amendment to civil service rules reads as follows (see Appendix A for full details).[2]

WHEREAS, Civil Service Rule I, Section 5-A(5) *Physical Standards For Firefighters* establishes physical standards that are required for appointment as Firefighter; and

WHEREAS, newly appointed Firefighters are not currently prohibited from smoking tobacco on or off duty; and

WHEREAS, it is appropriate to establish a no-smoking requirement for entry level Firefighters based on the City of Salem's liability as an employer under the State of Oregon's Occupational Disease Law (ORS 656.802) which presumes any disease of the lungs or heart contracted by a Firefighter after five years employment is the result of their employment.

NOW THEREFORE, BE IT RESOLVED that Rule 1, Section 5-A(5) be amended to read:

"Physical Standards for Firefighters.

5. Other   A. Normal physical condition as determined by the Medical Examiner's Report Form so as to be recommended for appointment.

B. Firefighters appointed after March 9, 1983 must not smoke tobacco either on or off duty during their term of employment."

ADOPTED BY THE Civil Service Commission this _____ day of _____, 1983.

In a related incident, Salem's police chief designated one small room as an exclusive smoking room under the city's general smokefree policy. Unfortunately, the room's ventilation system drew the smoke into several other offices, so that nonsmokers objected. The police chief ultimately banned smoking entirely in the building for police department employees. The other incident involved complaints by nonsmoking employees in the public works department in Salem about the more frequent breaks being taken by employees who smoke. This resulted in restriction of smoke breaks to the lunch hour and the two coffee breaks only.

The personnel director of Ft. Dodge, Iowa, wrote the authors that "because of the pension-related liability issue, we have discussed smoking as it relates to Police/Fire personnel." Several other jurisdictions also made similar comments about considering the nonsmoking issue for uniformed personnel because of the liability risks.

One suburban school district with 3,600 employees (classified and teaching), Davis County, Utah, based its no-smoking policy in all school buildings on a state statute (UCA 76-10-106, prohibiting smoking in school and other public buildings)—a law typical of most school systems in the United States. The district's policy handbook includes this very general statement:

No Smoking in School Buildings

A. Smoking in school buildings is prohibited by law. This regulation applies to students, teachers, maintenance personnel, administrators, visitors, personnel who rent school facilities, etc. The law has as its basis the necessity to prevent fire and/or explosion and their attendant effect on personnel, equipment, and buildings.

B. In view of the fact that students are prohibited from smoking on or near school grounds, it is respectfully requested that all school district employees refrain from smoking on school grounds as well as in school buildings.

The district's personnel director told the authors, "Smoking [is] not allowed in dining areas." This district *has* studied the smoking/nonsmoking issue as a means of containing health care costs and includes the issue in employee orientation and training.

As is true in most states, Utah regulates use or possession of tobacco products by minors (see UCA 76-10-105, making such "Possession of . . . Tobacco By Minors" a criminal offense). Utah has designated "compliance officers" in each school district (not teachers or students, but usually a vice principal) who enforce the nonsmoking policy on school grounds and in buildings. Accommodation in most general public buildings among public employees in Utah has been achieved by designating smoking/nonsmoking areas in cafeterias and so forth, but smoking is strictly prohibited in school buildings.[3]

Ramsey County, Minnesota (with over 5,000 employees), has had a smoking policy for many years (under Minnesota's "Clean Indoor Air Act") but has recently begun to enforce the provisions of the Act more rigorously for several reasons—moves into several new county office buildings have "forced employees to redefine work areas" and "come to grips with our preferences and dislikes"; "a number of incidents have arisen between smoking/nonsmoking employees which have forced supervisors to invoke provisions of the Act—which requires the preference of even *one* nonsmoker to be favored"; and because the county "made [an] internal study or research effort over the smoker/nonsmoker issue which led to greater emphasis on the enforcement of provisions of the earlier law." The ordinance defines floor areas, ventilation systems, complaints and appellate procedures, and so forth. It is of interest, however, that in one of the new county office buildings, the human services department has established a policy that "contains provisions that are beyond the minimum requirements established by the Minnesota Department of Health and the Minnesota Clean Indoor Air Act," as follows:

Smoking is prohibited throughout all CHSD leased space, except locations specifically designated as smoking permitted areas. Non-smoking areas include all offices whether occupied by one person or several, all open office areas, hallways, corridors, interview booths, conference rooms, restrooms, file areas and storage rooms. Portable ashtrays are banned from all non-smoking areas.

Smoking is permitted in specific designated and posted areas in waiting rooms, lounges, lunchrooms and shops. Employees are expected to confine smoking to normal rest breaks or lunch periods. Leaving a work area at any other time to participate in a break is not allowed. Nothing in this policy shall be construed to conflict with smoking prohibitions imposed by the Fire Marshal or other law, ordinances or regulations.

This departmental policy (which also provides for enforcement, penalties and appeals in other sections of the policy not quoted) embraces an area of concern, that smokers "get many more breaks and time away from their work area than nonsmokers"—that is, smokers leave their work areas more frequently than the normal two breaks per work shift. This same issue surfaces in a number of other places as well. The office of the deputy superintendent of the Oregon Department of Education (Salem, Oregon) issued a memorandum on November 7, 1979, to all staff, which addressed the department's policy on smoking breaks:

Supervisors shall allow smoking breaks for their employees which will be subtracted from the time designated for lunch. Also, employees needing more smoking time may take additional breaks by extending their working hours beyond the normal starting and ending times to ensure an eight-hour working day.

The personnel office of the city of Madison, Wisconsin, wrote the authors,

When the Wisconsin Clean Indoor Air Act [1983 Wisconsin Act 211, Non-Smoking Law] first passed in February 1983, the complete issue was clouded with rights' issues. After three years under the statute the air has cleared. We had a confrontation with union representatives who defended smokers rights—the next day nonsmoking union members demanded their rights be defended. This created political problems within the union itself.

Pasadena, California, in compliance with the above:

Gives nonsmokers incentives/advantages in lunchroom or cafeteria eating arrangements and separates smokers and nonsmokers in dining areas

Supports by internal promotion such yearly efforts as the "Great American Smokeout" sponsored by others as a national campaign

Provides or makes available programs to help city employees stop (or cut down on) smoking

Segregates smokers and nonsmokers in work areas or work stations or office/room assignment

Segregates smokers and nonsmokers in meeting rooms, conference rooms, training rooms, and so forth

Includes specific references to policy on smoking versus nonsmoking in pamphlets on health plans, medical coverage, employee fitness, employee assistance programs, and others

Posts signs in meal areas, restrooms, working areas

Several jurisdictions tried to help employees stop smoking (for health reasons) even where no other particular efforts were underway. Galesburg, Illinois, set up a "stop smoking clinic" in cooperation with a local hospital, for example.

The California State Personnel Board regulates approximately 144,000 public employees. The California Assembly passed a nonsmoking ordinance, which provides:

Each state department shall either adapt the existing policy of the State Personnel Board on smoking or adapt their own policy on smoking which addresses the rights of nonsmokers to a smoke-free environment in formal meetings, informal meetings and work stations, and which allows the administration of the policy and for the resolution of conflicts regarding the policy.

Many departments of California state government have now adopted their own nonsmoking policy under this 1982 law. For instance, the Contractors State License Board in Sacramento issued this bulletin to "all CSLB headquarters Building Employees" on January 6, 1986:

Subject: Headquarters Building No Smoking Policy

After considerable thought, analysis, and debate, a no-smoking policy has been developed for CSLB Headquarters building staff. The evidence that "secondary smoke" in most environments is hazardous to a non-smoking individual's health has become overwhelming. In addition, some people have allergic reactions to cigarette smoke. We ask that all employees abide by this no-smoking policy.

Effective January 13, 1986, there will be no smoking in the Headquarters work area. Smoking is acceptable in the break room; we are attempting to obtain purchase approvals for equipment to clear the smoke in this room. Those offended by smoking should plan to minimize their time in the break room until the equipment is purchased.

We recognize that this new policy may not be easy for some. We hope that supervisors will be flexible in the next few weeks to allow employees a few extra minutes to step away from work areas (to the break room or outside) if they just must smoke. This is for a transition period only and should not continue indefinitely.

I appreciate your cooperation in designing a healthier work environment.

The authors mailed (in 1986) 175 survey instruments to a random list of federal, state, and local governments; 145 usable responses were received for a response rate of 82 percent. In addition, dozens of respondents wrote letters or commentary and more than a score enclosed copies of policies, statutes, memoranda, and so forth. Many comments were extremely positive about the survey itself—obviously it aroused great interest.

Some 38 percent of the public agencies surveyed *did have* "formal or informal personnel policies and procedures on smoking versus nonsmoking at work." Based upon the data in the survey, of those responding "yes":

41.4%	Give nonsmokers incentives or advantages in lunchroom, dining room, cafeteria, or snack room seating or eating arrangements
24.1%	Give nonsmokers incentives/advantages in office or space assignments
20.7%	Give nonsmokers incentives or advantages in group life insurance, disability protection, or other nonmedical or health plan insurance provisions

6.9%   Give nonsmokers incentives or advantages in recruitment or initial selection for employment

7.0%   Give some other form(s) of incentives or advantages to nonsmokers (training, lower health plan premiums, and so on)

Of the repondents answering "yes" on the survey, some of the most common (over 75 percent of the responses) policies or procedures were:

11.7%   Respondents have a state law that covers at least some smoking policies

11.4%   Respondent's agency includes specific references to policy (on smoking versus nonsmoking) on the smoking/no smoking signs or posters displayed in working areas, meal areas, restrooms or lounges, or other work sites (other than where safety is a factor)

8.0%   Respondent's agency segregates smokers and nonsmokers in work areas or work stations or office or room assignments

8.0%   Respondent's agency provides or makes available programs (counseling, therapy groups, other formal means of employee assistance) to help employees stop (or cut down) on smoking

7.1%   Respondent's agency supports by internal promotion such yearly efforts as the "Great American Smokeout" sponsored by others as a national campaign

6.5%   Respondent's agency segregates smokers and nonsmokers in eating or dining areas

6.5%   Respondent's agency segregates smokers and nonsmokers in meeting rooms, conference rooms, training rooms, and so forth

6.5%   Respondent's agency provides "smokers' rooms" or a segregated, set-aside room (or rooms) where smokers are requested to go to smoke

5.9%   Respondent's agency includes specific references to policy on smoking versus nonsmoking in the employee handbook or policies and procedures manual

4.9%   Respondent's agency includes specific references to policy on smoking versus nonsmoking in new employee orientation

The smoking/nonsmoking issue in public agencies obviously leads to conflict between workers in the office and necessitates some form of intervention by management.

34.8%   Had an "incident" come up between smokers/nonsmokers where management had to intervene

24.4%   Designed an office or structured an office layout at least in part because of the smoking/nonsmoking issue

17.0%   Studied the smoking/nonsmoking issue while looking at ways to contain health care costs

11.9%   Made any kind of agency internal study or research effort over the smoker/nonsmoker issue

8.2%   Had an arbitration or grievance case over smoking/nonsmoking

1.5%   Had been involved in litigation with an employee over the smoking/nonsmoking issue

A number of interesting case studies were cited by respondents involving smoker/nonsmoker incidents, grievances, union relationship, or office layouts. Some of these cases are quoted below.

More than 77 percent of the survey respondents were nonsmokers (although some 25 percent of them were *former* smokers who had quit, one as recently as seven weeks before, others more than twelve years ago). These nonsmokers gave these primary reasons for *not* smoking: health reasons (44.2 percent); "messy" reasons—smell, stains, burns—(25.2 percent); cost factors (17.5 percent); religious reasons (4.9 percent); others—"never started," "didn't like the taste," "my children convinced me not to," and so on—(7.3 percent); and agency incentives or advantages (.9 percent).

Interestingly, 22.7 percent of the survey respondents themselves *were* smokers (78 percent smoked cigarettes; 9.3 percent smoked cigars; 9.3 percent smoked pipes; 3.1 percent used chewing tobacco). Smokers identified their own belief systems about the smoking/nonsmoking conflict as follows:

41.3%   I am personally willing to work or dine or visit in areas set aside at work for smokers.

33.3%   Problems in the work area between smokes and nonsmokers can best be solved by reasonable people conferring and compromising together and not by mandatory agency personnel policies and procedures.

12.7%   Whether an employee smokes is none of the employer's business (allowing for safety reasons, of course, such as fire hazards, danger around explosives, and so forth).

9.5%   The entire "secondhand smoke" controversy is overblown (no pun intended) and is not an issue where I work.

3.2%   Nonsmokers should *not* be given any agency incentives or advantages (for example, segregated dining areas, insurance advantages).

A number of smokers added written comments—one cigar smoker said cigars stink so badly that *he* doesn't even like to smoke them in an enclosed space; others were quite outspoken about what they perceive as a majority (nonsmokers) trampling on their (minority) rights. Several written comments expressed great reservations about proposed or actual restrictions on use of tobacco off the job: this was seen as a radical invasion of personal rights and privacy. In contrast, a number of nonsmokers added strong commentary about banning or restricting smoking in the workplace and passive, second-hand smoke: comments such as "it's about time"; "this is an issue whose time has come"; "we can measure the cost savings"; "I'm tired of being a passive smoker (sidestream smoke)"; and so forth. Not all written comments (on either side) showed polarization, but some expressed feelings and values were quite strong.

A Portland, Oregon, attorney requested a medical opinion on the "Health Effects of Cigarette Smoking and Relation of Such to Firemen."[4] The full medical opinion is reproduced in Appendix B to this chapter.

The Office of Personnel/Employee Relations for the Wisconsin Department of Transportation wrote that "it is clear there is no total concensus on implementing the [Nonsmoking Law], however, it is also evident that our employees realize that the intent of the law is to create a smoke-free environment." He added that departmental administrators met and agreed to the following policy:

1. All areas under the control of DOT will be considered non-smoking unless specifically designated as a smoking permitted area consistent with the law.

2. Break or lunch rooms may be designated as part smoking, and part non-smoking, and must be posted accordingly.

3. In those buildings where we have more than one lounge—some may be designated as smoking areas.

4. In those buildings where we have more than one restroom for each sex, some restrooms may be posted as smoking areas.

5. Offices—those with ceiling high partitions—may be posted as smoking areas.

6. In motor vehicles owned or operated for DOT, smoking is allowed if consented to by all occupants.

7. In those buildings that are controlled by DOT, the senior DOT managers are to work with the building superintendent to have part of the break and lunch rooms, lounges and restrooms designated as smoking areas. Consideration must be given to handicapped individuals.

8. The senior DOT managers at each location, except for the State Office Building and the Complex, are responsible for implementing this policy, and for the proper signing.

9. The Division of Business Management will coordinate the signing of the State Office Building and the Complex.

The director commented:

Strict enforcement of this policy is critical, as the law's intent is clear. We cannot afford anything less than uniform enforcement, since it would not be fair to smokers and non-smokers within other areas of the Department.

Signs designating the buildings as non-smoking, and those signs designating smoking areas, may be ordered through the Division of Business Management, Bureau of Management Services.

Every supervisor is responsible for uniform compliance consistent with this policy. Any violation shall be considered a violation of our work rules, and appropriate disciplinary action is to be taken.

Some local governments apply no-smoking rules even to municipal facilities that are leased, owned, or operated by the city. For instance, El Cajon, California, provides that,

A. The city manager shall be responsible for compliance with this chapter ["Prohibition of Smoking in Certain Public Areas"] when facilities which are owned, operated or leased by the City of El. Cajon are involved. The city shall provide business license applicants with a copy of this chapter.

B. The owner, operator or manager of any facility, business or agency shall post or cause to be posted all "No Smoking" signs required by this chapter. Owners, operators, managers or employees of same shall be required to orally inform persons violating this chapter of the provisions thereof. The duty to inform such violator shall arise when such owner, operator, manager or employee of same becomes aware of such violation.

C. It shall be the responsibility of employers to disseminate information concerning the provisions of this chapter to employees.

The mayor of Los Angeles established a 1985 smoking policy (Executive Directive No. 46) that regulated the following facilities to be designated as nonsmoking areas:

1. Restrooms.
2. Elevators.
3. Nurses-aid stations or similar facilities.
4. At least two-thirds of the seating capacity and floor space in cafeterias, lunchrooms, and employee lounges.

Work areas, including public counter areas, and departmental conference rooms, are to be regulated as follows:

1. Efforts shall be made by department managers to accommodate the desires of both smokers and non-smokers.

2. A smoke-free work area should be provided to non-smokers to the maximum extent possible, but expenses need not be incurred to make structural or physical modifications in providing these areas. Methods of accommodating the desires of smokers and non-smokers may include, but are not limited to, changing desk assignments, rearranging furniture, moving partitions, providing smokeless ashtrays, or improving ventilation. Such changes should not require relocation of electrical and telephone outlets or revisions to office lighting and air distribution systems.

3. Specific work areas may be designated as non-smoking areas.

4. Private enclosed offices occupied exclusively by smokers and all outdoor work areas are exempted from the above regulations.

But Mayor Tom Bradley added:

The City's policy is to emphasize cooperation between smokers and non-smokers. It is important to recognize that each work space is different and that regulation must be considered on a case by case basis. Employees and management are encouraged to seek fair and equitable accommodations and to resolve disputes in a spirit of compromise conducive to maintaining harmonious working relationships. It is expected that complaints regarding smoking can be handled by supervisors and most disputes between smokers and non-smokers resolved informally. Such policy, however, shall not preclude employees from filing formal grievances, where there are allegations that this Directive has been violated.

Any demand to meet and confer over implementation of this directive, received from any bona fide employee bargaining representative, shall be promptly referred to the City Administrative Officer for response.

Salt Lake County, Utah, offered classes, do-it-yourself cessation programs, hypnosis, and other efforts to assist its 3,000 or so county workers to quit smoking. See Appendix C for a complete list of such efforts at stopping smoking assistance programs (these are typical for many government agencies).

SUMMARY

An earlier survey of public agencies by the authors showed that some 38 percent of the public agencies (cities, counties, school districts, state agencies, and several federal agencies) *do* have smoking/nonsmoking policies.[5] Over 41 percent of the agencies with smoking policies segregated smokers and non-

smokers in dining or lunchroom areas; over 24 percent segregated smokers/
nonsmokers in office or space assignments; and over 20 percent favored nonsmokers in life and disability insurance programs. More than 75 percent of
those agencies with smoking policies included some form of reference to
smoking in policy manuals, included the topic in orientation and training, provided stop-smoking or therapy groups, or otherwise engaged in a wide variety
of other activities involving the smoking issue. Over 34 percent of the total
number of respondents have had an incident come up between smokers and
nonsmokers that required management intervention, and more than 24 percent reported designing an office or structuring an office layout at least in part
because of the smoking/nonsmoking issue. Some public jurisdictions now
restrict hiring to nonsmokers, including a few agencies that ban or restrict
smoking by their employees even off the job. Many other units are now
studying the smoking issue or plan to. Over 77 percent of the survey respondents were nonsmokers (a fourth of them, however, were former smokers).
Most of them did not smoke for health reasons and "messy" reasons (smell,
stains, burns)—their choice was rarely due to incentives or advantages offered
by management (.9 percent). Of the 22.7 percent of respondents who were
smokers, more than three-fourths smoked cigarettes, and over 18 percent
smoked pipes or cigars. Over a third of the smokers felt conciliation, compromise, and reasonableness could best solve workplace problems between
smokers and nonsmokers. A number expressed very strong feelings about the
erosion of smokers' "rights."

A number of cases are cited in this chapter of how various jurisdictions are
handling problem areas such as designating restricted areas, signs, smoking
"breaks" and relief periods, room ventilation, employee assistance programs,
hiring contracts, disability claims, and so forth.

In general, it appears that public jurisdictions, along with private industry,
will move at an accelerating pace toward a smokefree society in the years ahead.

NOTES

1. The above material and much of the following information is adapted from
William M. Timmins, "Smoking versus Nonsmoking at Work: A Survey of Public
Agency Policy and Practice," *Public Personnel Management* 16 (Fall 1987): 221-34.
See also "Hazardous Duty and Early Retirement: Some Policy Considerations,"
Pension Report 6 (July/August 1982): 9-10.

2. See also Appendix A to this chapter. It is Salem City's chief examiner's
"Memorandum to the Civil Service Commission" presented in its entirety.

3. "A Debate: Should [School] Districts Ban Smoking by Everyone on School
Premises?" *NEA Today* 6 (September 1987): 27.

4. Carl H. Lawyer to city attorney, letter dated January 28, 1983. Lawyer was a doctor with the Thoracic Clinic in Portland. Lawyer's letter was furnished to the authors by the fire chief of Salem City, Oregon. See Appendix B.

5. Timmins, "Smoking versus Nonsmoking at Work." A good example of the problems experienced with a local nonsmoking ordinance is found in John Seelmeyer, "Blood in the Office?" *Colorado Business* 13 (April 1986): 68-69.

Appendix A: Amendment to Civil Service Rule I, Section 5—Initiating a No-Smoke Requirement for Entry-Level Firefighters, Salem City, Oregon

ISSUE

An amendment to the Civil Service Rules is proposed to require that persons appointed as Firefighters after March 9, 1983 be non-smokers and remain so for the duration of employment as a firefighter with the City.

BACKGROUND

Staff has reviewed the physical qualifications for Firefighters at the time of appointment with particular attention to the liability of the City as an employer under Oregon's Occupational Disease Law (ORS 656.802). That law was adopted in 1961 and amended in 1977. It presumes that any firefighter employed more than five years who contracts any disease of the lungs or respiratory tract, hypertension or any cardiovascular-renal disease has contracted such disease(s) as a result of his employment and is therefore eligible for benefits under the Worker's Compensation Law. This presumption of compensability does not exist for any other occupation. It is commonly known as the "firefighter's presumption."

In all worker's compensation cases, except those involving firefighters, the claimant must provide medical evidence demonstrating that the disease or disability is related to his employment. In the case of a firefighter, however, the claimant is not required to produce such evidence. Only the five following facts need to be established to give rise to the firefighters' presumption of compensability:

1. Claimant has a disability or impairment of health, ORS 656.802(1)(b);

2. Claimant was employed as a firefighter of a political subdivision;

3. Claimant has completed more than five years of employment in such a capacity;

4. Claimant's disability or impairment was caused by a disease of the lung and/or cardiovascular system;

5. Claimant underwent a physical examination prior to his employment which failed to reveal any evidence of such condition of impairment of health which pre-existed his employment.

Once the presumption is established, the State Supreme Court has held in a 1982 decision (Wright v. SAIF) that the burden shifts to the insurer (or employer) to prove that the firefighter's condition is unrelated to his employment. In practical terms this means that medical evidence must be presented which overcomes the presumption of compensability and demonstrates that employment was not the cause of the condition. If this evidence is not conclusive, the statutory presumption requires that the claimant be ruled eligible for workers compensation benefits.

ANALYSIS

Diseases of the heart and lungs covered by this law are serious, sometimes fatal. The value of worker's compensation benefits granted to persons suffering form such diseases is therefore high. Factors taken into account in determining the amount of benefits awarded include future income during the balance of the claimant's working life which has been lost due to death or permanent disability, the number and age of the claimant's dependents, time-loss payments which may be made between the date of disability and the date when the condition is determined to be medically stable, and retraining costs which may be necessary to prepare the claimant for new employment consistent with his medical condition. In addition to these benefit costs, all medical expenses related to the treatment of the condition are paid by the insurer. While these factors differ for each claimant, the total value of benefits payable on any single claim can range from $60,000 to more than $400,000. Medical expenses can add between $1,000 and $600,000 to these amounts. Thus the total cost of a claim to the insurer may be well in excess of $100,000. As a self-insured employer, the City of Salem would pay all such costs directly, up to $150,000 per claim. Costs above that amount would be paid by an insurance company under an excess insurance policy purchased by the City to cover extraordinary losses.

Since 1974, at least three Salem firefighters have filed four claims under the firefighters' presumption. Each claimed to suffer from coronary heart disease. Three claims (two from one person) were denied; one claimant did not smoke, the other smoked 1½ packs daily. The claimant who did not smoke was determined in fact not to have coronary heart disease. The claimant who did smoke suffered from other health problems of overweight, high blood pressure and a hereditary history of coronary heart problems. His claims (2) were therefore denied by the Workers Compensation Boards and, on appeal, by the Circuit Court and Court of Appeals. Those claims were resolved before the law was amended in 1977 to clarify the basis for disputing the presumption and before the Supreme Court decision in Wright v. SAIF. If the claims were filed today they would have a greater chance of being sustained.

The third claimant smoked in excess of 1½ packs of cigarettes daily. He was awarded benefits and medical expenses totalling $59,254 to date. An additional $176,184 is reserved to pay future medical expenses which may be required and a lifetime monthly disability benefit of $901, approximately ⅔ of which would continued to be paid to his wife, if he is married, after his death. The claimant also received a job-related disability pension from the City's retirement plan of $747 per month for life. If the disability were not related to his job, the monthly pension would have been approximately $200.

Substantial medical evidence is available which documents the effects of smoking and employment in firefighting on cardiovascular and pulmonary diseases. Much of the evidence is discussed in the attached letters from Dr._____, a heart and lung specialist, and Dr._____, head of the Division of Cardiology at Oregon Health Sciences University [see Appendix B]. It is indisputable that persons who smoke are significantly more likely to contract the diseases which under state law are presumed to be related to firefighting employment for worker's compensation purposes. It is also established that at least three of those diseases (coronary heart disease, chronic obstructive pulmonary disease and excessive levels of carboxyhemoglobin) are major risk factors for firefighters. Just as persons who smoke are more likely to contract those diseases than are persons who don't smoke, firefighters are more likely to contract them than non-firefighters. Moreover, as Dr._____ points out, smoking and employment "would interact in a given fireman in an additive or multiplicative fashion to increase the risk of sustaining a disease if the fireman smokes cigarettes as well as having smoke exposure during fighting fires." Thus, firemen who smoke are more apt to contract these diseases than firemen who don't smoke.

Under the firefighters' presumption, the significantly higher probabilities of disease associated with both smoking and employment expose the insurer and employer to the unnecessary risk that a disease will be ruled compensable when it is in fact caused by smoking, not employment. When the firefighters' presumption has been established, the burden is on the insurer to improve that the disease is *not* related to employment. In practice, this may be impossible to document by medical evidence. Lawyer states that "It is not possible with pulmonary function equipment available, such as the spirometer, to distinguish between obstructive lung disease in firefighters caused by occupational exposure and obstructive lung disease caused by cigarette smoking if indeed there is in fact any difference in their lungs to be detected." Dr._____ states that it is very difficult to determine relative influence of several risk factors to the development of coronary disease in a given individual. Some success has been achieved with large groups but, he writes, "such studies . . . have not resolved the difficulty in determining the influence of a specific risk factor in individuals unless, . . . , there is one obvious major contribuitng risk factor." Clearly, for a firefighter who smokes there are at least two such risk factors and a determination of their relative influence would often be a matter of subjective opinion.

The City's exposure to claims ruled compensable under the firefighters' presumption can be reduced if fewer firefighters smoked because the incidence of cardiovascular and pulmonary diseases would decline. As a consequence, the potential costs of cases in which smoking is a major contributing factor would be avoided.

Several cities across the country have prohibited firefighters from smoking both on and off the job during their term of employment. The cities of Alexandria, Virginia, San Mateo, California and Eugene, Oregon have all adopted that regulation. In each case the prohibition was prompted by state laws containing some form of the firefighters' presumption for worker's compensation benefits. The regulation in Alexandria, Virginia was tested in federal court and upheld. The San Mateo regulation is being challenged in court now. The Eugene regulation has not faced legal challenge. All cities implemented the prohibition for new employees only and did not require existing employees to stop smoking.

Staff recommends that a prohibition against smoking be adopted for employees of the Salem Fire Department. Like the other cities, Salem should implement the policy for new firefighters only, effective March 9, 1983. Approximately one-third of the current work force, or about 45 employees, smokes. In our judgment, the long term risk posed by all future employees who may smoke is much greater than that posed by the smaller of number of current employees who smoke. The primary objective of this proposed policy, therefore, is to avoid the larger potential cost of benefits and medical expenses for the claims of future smokers.

This policy would be implemented through an employment agreement signed by new employees at the time of appointment in which they would acknowledge the prohibition against smoking on and off the job during the term of their employment. It would further provide that if they do smoke they would be subject to discipline, including termination.

We have asked the City Attorney's office to review this proposed policy and to advise us of its legality. Assistant City Attorney Jeannette Launer advises that there are no statutes or court cases which definitively establish the rights of employers and employees on this issue. However, it is her judgment that the policy is based on the legitimate municipal purpose of reducing costs to the employer and would be sustained on a "ratonal basis" test.

RECOMMENDATION

It is recommended that the Commission adopt Resolution No. 83-2 amending Section 5 of Civil Service Rule I to prohibit smoking during the term of employment of firefighters hired after March 9, 1983.

This proposed change in the existing Civil Service Rules was posted in the Fire Department on February 23, 1983 in accordance with Section 92A-5(b) of the City Charter and would become effective immediately upon adoption by the Commission.

Appendix B: A Medical Doctor Writes a City Attorney on Health Effects of Cigarette Smoking and Relation of Such to Firemen

Dear Attorney:

There are very important health effects for which a major risk factor is cigarette smoking, and an additional major risk factor are also exposures encountered by firemen. These would interact in a given fireman in an additive or multiplicative fashion to increase the risk of sustaining a disease if the fireman smokes cigarettes as well as having smoke exposure during fighting fires. These health effects include the following:

1. Coronary heart disease. Cigarette smoking is a major risk factor in all ages but is proportionately more important in heart attacks occurring in younger people. Cigarette smoking is responsible for 120,000 excess U.S. deaths from coronary heart disease each year (1). A study of Los Angeles firefighters indicated a high prevalence of ischemic heart disease remaining elevated after a risk factor analysis, including correction for cigarette smoking, was performed (2). Other studies indicated an excessive risk of coronary heart disease in firemen not explained by cigarette smoking have been published.

2. Risk of obstructive lung disease. Obstructive lung disease, known as COPD or chronic obstructive pulmonary disease, includes chronic bronchitis and pulmonary emphysema. Cigarette smokers have four to twenty-five times the risk of death from these diseases as nonsmokers. Damage is seen in lungs of even young smokers of cigarettes. Non-cigarette smoking firemen can also sustain obstructive lung disease, occurring sometimes in an acute several fulminate fashion after acute exposure to smoke. The smoke in these cases is often from burning plastics, and in some cases the exposure follows the fireman being trapped for a time in a burning building with a "smoke out." There are reports in the medical literature of this condition, and I have in my personal pulmonary medicine practice evaluated at least two patients with the

condition. One was a firechief with repeated exposures, and the other a worker who had a single exposure to burning plastic material in a wastebasket over about a 20-minute period and sustaining a severe disabling obstructive lung disease, having been previously a healthy nonsmoker. It is known that burning plastics can generate phosgene which when it interacts with the moisture lining the air tubes in the lungs produced hydrochloric acid and a burning of the tissues leading to scarring and the obstructive lung condition. Oxides of nitrogen such as NO_2 can also be produced and produce nitric acid on acting with the water [in the tissues], and are a known cause of obstructive lung disease with acute exposures. A study published by A. W. Musk et al., in the *British Journal of Industrial Medicine*, 1979, volume 36, pages 29 to 34, "Pulmonary functions in firefighters—acute changes in ventilatory capacity and their correlates" found decreases in FEV-1 of up to 500 ml. with smoke exposure by firefighters. The FEV-1 is the "forced expiratory volume in one second" and is measured by having the subject blow as hard and as fast as he can after a full inspiration into a device known as a spirometer. The volume of air blown out in the first second is then termed the FEV-1 and reflects the amount of airway obstruction, being reduced in the presence of obstructive lung disease. In this study the decline in FEV-1 was related to the severity of the smoke exposure as estimated by the firefighter and to the major particulate concentration of the smoke to which he was exposed. Changes in FEV-1 resulting from a second exposure to smoke on the same shift were greater when smoke exposure in the previous fire was heavy. The study concludes "repeated episodes of irritation of the bronchial tree that have been documented in this investigation may explain the origin of the previously observed chronic effects of firefighting on respiratory symptoms and pulmonary function." Other references are important studies by Peters showing an abnormal degree of airway obstruction in firefighters after correction for cigarette smoking. These important references are Peters et al., "Chronic effect of firefighting on pulmonary function," *New England Journal of Medicine*, 1914, Volume 291, page 1320-1322, 1974, and Sidor and Peters, *American Review of Respiratory Disease*, Volume 109, pages 255-261, "Prevalence rates of chronic nonspecific respiratory disease in firefighters." I note that many of the studies, including that by Musk, et al., were performed when members of the Boston Fire Department were using a self-contained breathing apparatus for personal protection when smoke conditions were "perceived to be dangerous." The above studies documented not only an excess yearly decline in FEV-1 but also chronic mucous hypersecretion in non-cigarette smoking firefighters. It is not possible with pulmonary function equipment available, such as the spirometer, to distinguish between obstructive lung disease in firefighters caused by occupational exposure and obstructive lung disease caused by cigarette smoking if indeed there is in fact any difference in their lungs to be detected.

3. The third risk of cigarette smoking relates to elevation of carboxyhemoglobin level in the blood. Inhaled carbon monoxide in smoke of any kind, including that from cigarette smoking, diffuses into the blood stream and combines with the hemoglobin in the red blood cells. It forms a compound known as carboxyhemoglobin which is very stable and only slowly diffuses back out of the blood. Normal

subjects in urban America will have about 1 to 2% carboxyhemoglobin and a moderate cigarette smoker approximately 8% carboxyhemoglobin. The above study by Musk et al. showed that non-cigarette smoking firemen after fighting fire had an average of 6 parts per million carboxyhemoglobin whereas in current cigarette smokers it averaged 15 parts per million. "Subtle changes of central nervous system function have been consistently demonstrated at the 5 to 10% carboxyhemoglobin level (e.g., increased visual threshold, impaired higher cognate function)." In addition, precipitation of anginal episodes (chest pain due to heart disease) has been noted in patients during exercise with carboxyhemoglobin levels of 3 to 5% (3). Thus, a cigarette smoking fireman is more likely with exposure while fighting a fire to have elevation of his carboxyhemoglobin level into the range where significant impairment in decision making, coordination and timing, and temporal impairment and visual impairment would occur.

The following risks of cigarette smoking are not to my knowledge risks that are also increased in nonsmoking firemen, at least in that I am not aware of scientific medical studies showing such. Thus confusion as to etiology and compensability would seem less likely.

1. Lung cancer, the most common form of cancer in men and an increasingly common form in women, has as its major cause cigarette smoking.

2. Larynx cancer is 2.9 to 17.7 times more frequent in smokers, including pipe and cigar smokers, than in nonsmokers.

3. Cancer of the esophagus is 2 to 9 times more frequent in smokers of cigarettes, pipes or cigars, particularly if they drink alcohol.

4. Bladder cancer is 7 to 10 times more likely in cigarette smokers than nonsmokers.

5. Cancer of the pancreas is 2 to 5 times more likely in cigarette smokers.

6. Cigarette smokers get more peptic ulcers and die more often of them.

7. Risk of sudden death is approximately 2½ times more likely in a one-pack-a-day smoker than in a nonsmoker.

Thus, in summary the effects on coronary heart disease, obstructive lung disease, and elevation of carboxyhemoglobin level interfering cognitive function all occur to a significant degree from cigarette smoking, and occur to a significant degree in non-cigarette smoking firemen. Of course, the other undesirable health effects of smoking such as cancer, from which approximately 350 Americans die every day, make cigarette smoking undesirable in anyone (4).

Sincerely,

_____, M.D.
Thoracic Clinic
Portland, Oregon 97213

1. "Dangers of smoking, benefits of quitting, and relative risks of reduced exposure," revised edition, American Cancer Society, 777 Third Avenue, New York, NY 10017, copyright 1980.

2. Barnard RJ: "Ischemic heart disease in firefighters of normal coronary arteries," *Journal of Occupational Medicine,* 18:818, 1976.

3. Beeson & McDermott: *Textbook of Medicine,* page 63, 1975.

4. Surgeon General's report "Health consequences of smoking—cancer," 1982. Office of Smoking, U.S. Dept. of Health & Human Services, Rockville, Maryland 20857.

Appendix C: Salt Lake County Employee Smoking Cessation Programs

A. *Classes*

1. American Cancer Society—322-0431—"FreshStart"
   Two 1 hour sessions a week for 2 weeks—$20

2. Utah Lung Association—484-4456—"Freedom from Smoking"
   Held at St. Mark's Hostpital—268-7422 (SLC)
   and St. Benedict's Hospital—479-2016 (Ogden)
   Eight 2 hour weekly sessions $35

3. LDS Hospical—321-1004
   3-4 hours of individual counseling-$25

4. Seventh Day Adventist program—484-4331
   Held at Wasatch Hills Church, 2139 Foothill Dr. SLC
   Five 1½ hour sessions in 5 consecutive days—(Fri.-Tue.)—$15

5. University of Utah "Change Clinic"—581-7002
   Seven 1½ hour weekly sessions + 3-4 maintenance sessions
   (preparation + 2 weeks of withdrawal before "quit day")

6. Utah Department of Health—533-6141—"I Can Quit"
   Modeled on the University of Utah program Seven 1½ hour weekly
   sessions + 3-4 maintenance sessions (preparation + 2 weeks of withdrawal before "quit day") Assistance in implementing worksite
   programs

7. Cottonwood Hospital—262-3461 (Nanette)
   Every 2 months
   Next class: March 4 (7 sessions) (7 weeks)
   Handouts and tapes—$35

B. *Do It Yourself*

   1. American Cancer Society—322-0431   Free pamphlet

   2. Utah Heart Association—322-5601   Free pamphlet

   3. Utah Lung Association—484-4456   2 booklets:—$7
      "Freedom from Smoking in 20 Days"
      "A Lifetime of Freedom from Smoking"

   4. Nicorette gum (prescription drug) + Physician counseling

C. *Hypnosis*

   1. Utah Lung Association—484-4456
      One 2 hour session teaches self-hypnosis—$35

   2. Private therapist
      Initial 2-hour session—$45 (approx.)
      Follow-up 1 hour session—$25 (approx.)

Appendix D: Smoking Cessation Programs
Outside Salt Lake County

1. McKay-Dee Hospital Center, Ogden (Women's Center): Jean 627-2800
   6 week program sponsored by American Cancer Society
   Women only—$30

2. St. Benedict's Hospital, Ogden—Rick Knowlton—479-2016
   "Freedom from Smoking"—8 week program, built-in maintenance/$40

3. Brigham City Community Hospital—Kay Peterson—734-9471
   "FreshStart"

4. Logan Regional Hospital—752-2050 Ext. 119
   Cessation program begins in March (Tues. & Thurs.—4 weeks)
   For corporation worksite cessation programs, contact: Diane Tracy—752-2050

5. Castleview Hospital (Price)—637-4800—Jim Piacetelli

6. Smith Clinic (373-8660) Provo
   Paul and Charles Smith (M.D.s)
   5 Day Stop Smoking Plan
   $30—rebate offered
   Classes held at Utah Valley Hospital and Seventh Day Adventist Church

7

THE RESPONSE BY PRIVATE FIRMS

In 1987 the prestigious Bureau of National Affairs and the American Society for Personnel Administration reported that 54 percent of the private firms they surveyed currently had a smoking policy, and 4 percent more were considering such a policy (most existing policies had been adopted within the past few years). The greatest number of those businesses with a smoking policy provided for a total ban on smoking in all open work areas. Most policies encouraged employees to resolve problems themselves.[1] This chapter independently surveys private sector practice now current in the United States, including some detailed information on a number of successful efforts.

Mountain View Hospital is an investor-owned (for profit) hospital in Payson, Utah—part of a multi-hospital system called Health Trust, Inc. (more than 100 hospitals nationally). It operates under a board of directors and a CEO. In April of 1988 the hospital went nonsmoking.

Two major hospitals dominate the central Utah market: Mountain View and a large medical center some ten miles away. Mountain View has become one of the most successfully managed and profitable hospitals in the HTI system. Still, competition is characteristic of the health care market: Several new emergency centers and group clinics have opened in nearby communities and the hospital has had to become highly competitive (quality, price, care and services, responsiveness to physicians and patients) to survive, let alone thrive, in the new marketplace. The decision to go nonsmoking was seen as part of this competitive edge.

Obviously, hospitals should be health oriented, and nonsmoking is perceived by the general public as a health issue. The CEO, at the request of the governing board, made a study of "going nonsmoking" throughout the hospital. Interviews by the CEO with the medical staff and the medical staff executive committee (elected by the physicians) revealed that 80 percent or more of the physicians were nonsmokers and supported the concept. The doctors' primary concern was what the impact of a nonsmoking policy would be on patients. While most admissions to a hospital result from the decision of the physicians, patient preferences still play a large role. If enough patients objected to the proposed policy, physicians would be forced to admit them elsewhere (and the major competitor was only a few minutes away). Doctors on the medical staff who smoked raised few objections, surprisingly. Much of the hospital was already off-limits to smoking, including surgery and intensive care units, and nearly every doctor who smoked was already careful about where he or she lit up: never in a patient's room or waiting areas, for example, and with discretion in the physician's lounge and the cafeteria.

The CEO and staff surveyed a sample of clients—patients from the entire market area served by the hospital. Those surveyed included past admissions, those being admitted, those already in the hospital, and those who might use the hospital in the future. Interestingly, more than three-fourths of the public strongly supported the idea of a nonsmoking hospital: The response was over-whelmingly enthusiastic. Even smokers supported the idea if exceptions could be allowed on a case-by-case basis with the patient and physician. Indeed, the public survey suggested going nonsmoking would improve the hospital's image and increase its competitive edge.

Members of the governing board (trustees) spent some time talking with persons of influence in the market area. The trustees represented many of the major employers in the region (one with some 20,000 employees), including one trustee who was a prominent local elected official. No negative feedback resulted. Rather, several major national corporations with local facilities expressed support because they were considering a nonsmoking policy them-selves, usually for health care cost containment reasons. One trustee was the manager for a major food processing firm and his company totally restricted smoking on the job because of product sanitation. Several times during the study the policy was an agenda item for the governing board, so that some trustee discussion took place over a period of months.

Meetings with employees produced some polarization: A few employees felt "it was about time" the hospital went nonsmoking; the 10 to 15 percent who smoked were less than enthusiastic and felt it was unfair. From the beginning the policy was explained as an employee health issue and as making the hospital totally smokefree—no smoking by workers or visitors anywhere in the building and no smoking at entrances and public areas. Smoking by employees would be restricted to outside the buildings and in only a few specific areas not readily visible to patients or the public.

Ultimately, by the time the CEO brought the proposed nonsmoking policy to the governing board for approval, a modification had been made: Patients could smoke in their rooms (a few rooms were set aside for this purpose) if their attending physician wrote a prescription authorizing tobacco products. This was the policy adopted.

Since implementation the results have been quite measurable.

- The hospital's market share has increased. It would be too easy to attribute this solely to the nonsmoking policy, but along with all other marketing strategies the new nonsmoking policy appears to have helped the hospital to win a bigger piece of the highly competitive local and regional market.

- Press coverage has been quite positive. The number of column inches in local papers that commented on the new policy is impressive and entirely favorable (the hospital early on made the decision to "go public," to be highly visible with the nonsmoking policy, and not to downplay or minimize the policy).

- The personnel officer reports no significant problems in worker recruitment or retention. At least one grievance was filed (and promptly resolved by the immediate supervisor) and several worker complaints continue to surface, especially when weather is bad because smokers must literally smoke out in the wind and rain (or go to their automobiles). Personnel reports several supervisors have had problems enforcing uniform times for breaks and lunch (smokers take longer and more frequent breaks—this is resented by nonsmokers, she says). Even recruiting nurses (where there exists both a national and regional shortage of serious proportions) does not seem to be hampered by the nonsmoking policy (personnel and the director of nursing carefully explain the policy to all applicants).

- The hospital facilities director says his records already indicate real cost savings in room maintenance (cleaning of drapes, linens, waste receptacles, carpets) and in maintenance of restrooms and public areas. For instance, the maternity waiting room always posed a serious cleaning and ventilation problem (from some expectant fathers who smoked). This was completely resolved. Careful placement of receptacles for smoking materials and signs at entrances and inside the building have meant minimal additional grounds maintenance. One interesting note was the improvement in air quality throughout the hospital—air filters are not as dirty, etc. The facilities director is a nonsmoker but many of his crews smoke. He admits he must play an active surveillance role and dislikes the role of enforcer—but "it goes with his title."

- Patient surveys reveal high levels of satisfaction with the new policy—at least among nonsmokers. But even smokers who were surveyed expressed some positive attitudes; the hospital is in the health business, after all. Very few, if any, cases can be demonstrated where a patient selected another hospital or facility solely because of the nonsmoking policy. So few patients have asked their physicians for a prescription to smoke in their hospital rooms that the CEO and director of the medical staff couldn't recall *any* specific cases but allowed as there "had been a few." The medical staff see the new policy as a non-issue.

- The hospital recognized some workers might want to cut down on their smoking or to quit altogether in light of the new policy. So a number of smoking cessation programs were sponsored for workers on a low cost basis (some charge is typically considered as necessary in such efforts to provide a commitment by the smoker). These programs were conducted by experienced MDs and psychiatric staff on a counselling, self-help basis. Few smoking employees took part but some did successfully "kick the habit" and others reduced their use of tobacco. No other incentives, however, were offered. The hospital has offered such courses (plus weight reduction, dietary control, etc.) for years to the community as a whole. Such courses usually attract small numbers of dedicated people and actively involve the hospital with various groups in the community.

- The governing board reviewed the results of the policy after the first few months and found results uniformly so good that no changes are currently [1988] proposed in the nonsmoking policy at the hospital.

Mountain View Hospital's adoption of a nonsmoking policy must be judged a success. Why? Chapter 8 gives a number of implementation recommendations (and examples of written policies). It would appear the hospital carefully followed such recommendations and has also documented the successful results.

Being a proprietary business in a highly competitive local market makes the hospital a bit sensitive to the release of some cost and market penetration data, but enough information can be documented to show "going nonsmoking" has proven a successful policy for this well-run and profitable hospital.

As of 1988 only 8 percent of U.S. hospitals had banned smoking, but 90 percent of hospitals (for profits, not for profits, religious, and community) already restricted smoking to designated places in their facilities. The American Hospital Association (AHA) in Chicago provides a free communications kit for hospitals called "Smoking and Hospitals Are a Bad Match," which outlines the next steps for hospitals and others. The U.S. Health Care Financing Administration (HCFA) had advised the AHA that the government may use its "regulatory clout" to force hospitals to ban smoking in their facilities. The agency wrote hospital administrators in 1988 encouraging them to "work toward achieving a totally smoke-free environment as quickly as possible." HCFA urged hospitals to voluntarily take steps now to preempt further action from HCFA.[2]

A survey by the American College of Healthcare Executives (Chicago) asked hospitals, "What incentives, if any, have you offered your employees to participate in health promotion activities?" Responses were:[3]

Time off to attend class/program	55%
No charge for class/program	71%
Subsidy (either partial or full) for offsite program	32%
Bonus for participants	5%
None of the above	15%
Other (please specify)	5%

Some businesses are very critical of mandatory nonsmoking laws, however. For instance, the president of the New York Restaurant Association considers New York's restrictions on smoking in restaurants as placing the restaurant owner in the position of the police officer, confronting patrons who come to dine and making the owner the enforcer of an unpopular law.[4] Victor Rosellini, former president of the National Restaurant Association, argued that nonsmoking restrictions (now enforced in some dozen states) "inconvenience customers, force operators to police their own establishments, reduce profits and even result in costly lawsuits." South Carolina Senator Thomas E. Smith, Jr., estimated that New York's 1988 law would cost restaurants "as much as $17,000 per establishment" to comply with the restrictions and result in a 10 percent unemployment figure.

Rosellini stated that waiters and waitresses wanted to be friendly and efficient and earn tips, not be "nonsmoking hall monitors" and risk offending patrons. Busy restaurants often had to make smokers wait when mandatory smoking space was empty, and often owners start "bending rules" rather than lose or offend customers in a highly competitive business.

The National Restaurant Association has published a brochure on establishing a nonsmoking section—it covers a number of areas such as posting signs, accommodating everyone, monitoring usage patterns, use of air cleaners, training service personnel, and seeing opportunities rather than problems. NRA's 1985 survey showed 21 percent of its members had nonsmoking sections. Still, most owners preferred to respond to customer demand than to state or local legislation.

In general, the restaurant industry is fighting government regulation of their industry—they want to regulate themselves. Surveys show most people will patronize a restaurant without a nonsmoking section, even though they prefer nonsmoking dining.

In 1986 the Safety Science Department of the University of Southern California surveyed ninety-eight hotel and motel chains on setting aside nonsmoking rooms for guests.[5] Forty-one chains responded: Most have nonsmoking guest rooms, the allocation ranging from 5 to 30 percent of their rooms being set aside as nonsmoking rooms (typically the allocation is 10 percent). Usually guests were informed of the policy at check-in, by listings in hotel directories, lobby signs, reservations centers, ads in Yellow Pages, and in-flight magazines.

Most of the chains responded that the nonsmoking guest room concept has been quite successful (21 percent) or has posed "no problems" (24 percent). A number of chains planned to increase the number of nonsmoking rooms (17 percent). The "worst problem" cited was unavailability of a nonsmoking room for nonsmokers, who were disappointed if such rooms weren't available upon request. The survey concluded that providing 10 to 30 percent of nonsmoking rooms was "good business" and projected "the trend will be toward higher percentages in the future."

A somewhat related view is expressed by Don S. Johnson in an editorial for *Administrative Management* (vol. 47, February 1986: 9) in which Johnson points out he is a life-long pipe smoker and part of some 51 million Americans who smoke—almost a third of the adult population. "That," he says, "is a lot of potentially good workers to discriminate against with a 'don't hire a smoker' policy." Forcing smokers not to smoke on the job may, Johnson points out, diminish smokers' creativity, make them more irritable, more easily distracted, lower overall smoker productivity, and even force them to break the rules by cheating. Johnson strongly opposes smokefree workplaces and favors "accommodations for smokers and nonsmokers alike."

Johnson does not address the issue of companies helping their workers to quit smoking—smoking cessation programs. Chapter 6 reviewed a number of public sector efforts in this regard. But the private sector has been quite active as well (as in the hospital example above). Pacific Northwest Bell, which employs 15,000 people in three states, offered free smoking cessation courses for several years and "only 331 people" took the free classes. During the first two years of the company's total smoking ban, however, over 1,800 employees and spouses signed up.[6] Pacific Northwest Bell reimbursed employees (and family members) for the costs of whatever cessation program was chosen.

When Pacific Northwest Bell first adopted its smoking policy it outlawed smoking in meeting rooms and the largest share of their cafeterias and allowed groups to decide whether to ban smoking. After two years of problems (union grievances over disparate treatment in the company's 750 buildings, complaints about "passive" smoke, and other enforcement problems) the company adopted a complete smoking ban in all its facilities.[7] The parent company, US West, is considering going smokefree by 1989. In a telephone interview (June 16, 1988) a Pacific Northwest representative told the authors of some of the problems that prompted the total ban: One, the company was receiving many letters from workers in the hundreds of buildings complaining about disparate treatment; two, quality of working life committees were regularly unable to resolve the conflicts between different work groups whose policies were more lenient or more strict; and, three, many grievances were filed (by smokers and nonsmokers alike)—just one floor supervisor in a main office building had some 150 grievances filed in a short period; it was impossible to resolve all the conflicts by accommodation. A complete ban was seen as the only answer. At Pacific Northwest the nonsmoking effort was a true "grass roots" movement and the union played a critical role in selling it to top management. Top officers went along because of the overwhelming union support and the convincing case on employee health and fitness (costs and benefits).

Pacific Northwest considered incentives but discarded the idea as unnecessary (other than reimbursing the cost of smoking cessation classes). Unions wanted the smoking policy to be added to the existing company employee assistance program (smoking was seen as addictive as alcohol or other drugs). Problems of smokers abusing time allowed for rest breaks has been partly ameliorated by the fact that many workers are on flex-time, so longer or more frequent breaks can be more easily handled.

Texas Instruments employs 75,000 employees in 150 countries. In 1986 TI went smoke free in all its U.S. locations: Smoking was allowed only in specially designated lounges for the 20,000 employees in the United States and Canada.[8] At TI there was a tenfold increase in the number of employees who signed up for smoking cessation classes once the company ban went into effect.[9]

LeRoux reports that Bonne Bell, Inc., of Lakewood, Ohio, awards a $250 incentive to employees who quit smoking for at least six months after signing up for the company's smoking cessation program. Backsliders must pay $500 to a local charity.[10] City Federal Savings and Loan of Birmingham, Alabama, goes a step further: Smokers who quit get a $20 monthly bonus "for as long as they do not smoke." Most of the Savings and Loan's workers receive the bonus. The plan has been in operation for more than 20 years.[11]

In a telephone interview with the authors (June 16, 1988), a public relations officer at City Federal explained that the policy is outlined in the employee handbook, simple and short: Abstain for thirty days or longer on and off the job and you qualify for the bonus; backslide and lose the bonus. The $20 a month is added in as a taxable benefit, not as part of an employee's base pay (so is not computed into pension and other contributory amounts). Over more than two decades of experience with the policy the company has been able to rely upon personal integrity to police total abstinence. Very few incidents have arisen over employees who cheat on the policy (smoking but still collecting the bonus), but one such recent incident led to a discharge of a worker—her lack of personal integrity was seen as risky in a financial institution. The $20 a month has not been changed since the beginning of the program (started by one of the founders of the institution) and is still judged an adequate incentive: More than 300 of the 400 employees are receiving the bonus. The program is perceived as very popular with City Federal's employees.

Typical of numerous insurers, Blue Cross and Blue Shield of Minnesota offer significant reductions of premiums on health coverage to groups of nonsmokers (as much as 29 percent). Such incentives can provide real impetus to smoking cessation efforts. The reverse is also true: higher premiums are being sought for older smokers who persist in smoking.[12]

USG Corp., Chicago, hires 1,300 workers in nine plants who handle mineral fibers and are at risk of lung disease or lung cancer. The company banned smoking by these workers on or off the job in 1987. USG hires over 23,000 other workers at other sites where the ban does not apply.[13] The firm has been involved in thousands of lawsuits in recent years, settling over 3,200 personal injury suits by the end of 1985 alone. The ban has attracted negative comment by many but others see the firm as laying a solid legal groundwork for future defense against liability, applying the costly lessons it learned in the earlier mass of litigation. Critics see USG's policy as virtually impossible to enforce off the job.[14]

William McManus, group vice president at USG, told the authors on June 16, 1988, that initially 300 or 400 workers signed up for smoking cessation classes. Spouses were encouraged to attend as well. The company felt this effort was an unqualified success. Individual workers can still get help upon request but the original cessation effort has run its course. McManus feels the media has blown USG's position all out of proportion (from critical essays on civil rights in *Penthouse* to cartoons and jibes in the Chicago newspapers). No effort was ever intended to snoop into people's private lives or to police employee compliance off the job. Supervisors counsel workers and remind them of the policy as needed. The company admits that a few grievances have been filed but all were resolved at informal stages.

Federal Express corporation, with some 50,000 employees nationwide, banned smoking in all its vehicles, airplanes, and buildings by 1988. The company took two years to phase in the program to become a smokefree company.[15] In a telephone interview with a public relations officer on June 15, 1988, the authors were told the phase-in went smoothly and there has been a minimum of problems. Cost and safety considerations played a big role in the ban on smoking in vans and delivery vehicles and airplanes, but employee health (and cost containment) was the primary objective overall.

Lincoln National Corporation of Fort Wayne, Indiana, hired over 3,500 workers in 1988. The company banned all smoking in the home office more than two years ago. An April 24, 1985 "News Flash" put out by Lincoln National emphasized the "concern for its employees' health." By 1986 the "Company News" for February 1 explained the designated smoking areas had been "a good first step, but it hasn't been enough," and announced the new nonsmoking policy. Lincoln National is an insurance holding company and was primarily concerned with its image in the health insurance industry, as well as with individual employee health. Nettie Nice, employee relations director, advised the authors (on June 16, 1988) that no serious complaints or problems have arisen over the smoking ban. Lincoln has chosen to settle conflicts that may arise by prompt action by individual managers and supervisors. The company has had no layoffs or discharges over the smoking ban, although they readily acknowledge problems do come up. The most serious issue has been charges by nonsmokers that smokers abuse the "twenty minutes per day" break time allowance. Individual managers are expected to work these conflicts out by counseling and efforts at accommodation. Workers who smoke must leave the building to do so but are asked not to congregate around main entrances (for "image" reasons). Other entrances do have roof overhangs, but the company admits it is not unusual to see smokers standing outside under an umbrella in inclement weather. The company has had some very vocal critics but most employees enthusiastically support the ban. No consideration was ever given to incentives (say, a cash bonus)—they were never seen as necessary. Initially, Lincoln National offered smoking cessation programs (spouses included) and "hundreds" signed up. Two years later the company no longer offers such programs ("no need exists") but will assist individuals on a case-by-case basis. The smoking policy is clearly described in the company employee handbook and is covered in new employee orientation. An employee newsletter called "Priorities" (for September 1985) encouraged attendance at smoking cessation classes and emphasized, "please remember that these classes could be very good use of company time." Classes were conducted at several locations, dates, and times and were made as convenient as possible.

Lincoln National's representative told the authors of two ongoing efforts to resolve questions that still arise over the smoking ban. First, questions on the smoking policy are regularly answered in the employee newsletter, and the company's CEO always is asked at least a few questions on the ban by employees during the annual open forum for all workers. Lincoln is "open, forthright, and honest" in responding to such questions and complaints. The CEO, however, is a strong booster of the ban and was proud to receive the distinguished "Benjamin Franklin Award" for his efforts to ban smoking.[16]

While only a few companies have adopted a policy of hiring *only* nonsmokers, those who have seem satisfied. Easton Aluminum (Van Nuys, California) includes the "nonsmokers only" policy in its advertising for vacancies, on its application blank, policy manual, orientation sessions, and so forth. Beginning in 1988 the firm of about 1,300 employees hired only nonsmokers for its new distribution center, and by 1989 the policy will extend companywide. At least one warehouse worker was discharged for violating the policy: He was caught smoking in a restroom but had stated he was a nonsmoker at the time of employment. The company admits it will ultimately have a dual standard—long-tenured workers who can smoke off the job (smoking will be banned at all company facilities) and new hires (after 1988) who must be nonsmokers on or off the job. Eventually, all employees will be nonsmokers as people retire or quit. The president of the company is a great believer in physical fitness (they manufacture many popular lines of sporting goods) and has dual motives for the ban. The company has clearly announced its intentions and has seen great employee interest in the company's smoking cessation programs being offered in advance of the total ban.

A survey by a national chemical producers trade journal, *Chemical and Engineering News* 66 (March 18, 1987): 16-17, reported that

corporate reaction to the concern over smoking ranges widely. Some employers such as Air Products & Chemical, Hoechst Celanese, Dow Chemical, 3M, Allied-Signal, GAF, PPG Industries, and Rohm & Haas have clear prohibitions against smoking in office environments. However, others such as DuPont, Union Carbide, Hercules, and Ethyl Corp. have no stated smoking policies. Monsanto straddles the line; only its agricultural division at St. Louis headquarters has smoking prohibitions in public areas.

The trade journal concludes that "the trend is toward more smoking restrictions in chemical company offices."

The appendix to this chapter provides a number of detailed documents on Pacific Northwest Bell's (now US West Communications) nonsmoking program.

NOTES

1. "Smoking in the Workplace," *ASPA-BNA Bulletin to Management* 51 (November 25, 1987): 1-12.

2. One of the authors served as chairperson of the board of Mountain View Hospital for several years and writes this case from this perspective. Also, "HCFA Strongly Urges Hospital Smoking Ban," *AHA News* 24 (June 13, 1988): 2. See also two 1988 case studies published (photocopies) by the American College of Health-care Executives, Chicago, "University of Chicago Medical Center" and "St. Cloud Hospital, St. Cloud, Minnesota," each called "Hospital Smoking Policies: Case History," for related examples. ACHE issued a "Public Policy Statement: Health Promotion and Prevention" in July 1985, using smoking cessation programs by hospitals as part of "maintaining and enhancing a healthy lifestyle."

3. Survey released in 1988 by the American College of Healthcare Executives, Chicago.

4. "Survey: No-Smoking Rooms Here to Stay," *Hotel and Motel Management* 201 (May 19, 1985): 1, 18-19.

5. This and material immediately following is adapted from Jean E. Palmieri, "Profits Go Up in Smoke When Nonsmoking Sections Are Mandatory," *Nation's Restaurant News* 20 (February 24, 1986): F7; Laurie Bain, "Where There's Smoke, There's Legislation," *Restaurant Business* 86 (August 10, 1987): 122-28; and James E. Peters, "The No-Smoking Controversy Heats Up," *Restaurant Business* 85 (September 20, 1986): 120-23.

6. Margaret LeRoux, "Companies Aiding Smokers Who Want to 'Kick the Habit,' " *Business Insurance* 20 (September 29, 1986): 64-65; also, Leonard D. Beil, "Pacific Northwest Bell's Approach to Implementing a No-Smoking Policy," *Modern Job Safety and Health Guidelines* (October 14, 1987): 28-31.

7. James Braham, "Ban It or Restrict It?" *Industry Week* 235 (November 30, 1987): 16-17. Tim Falconer, "No Butts About It," *Canadian Business* 60 (February 1987): 66-70 discusses ideal ways to handle smoker's break times, cessation incentives, ventilation problems, and so forth.

8. "Case Report 2: Texas Instruments," *Personnel Management*, 20 (January, 1988), pp. 48-49.

9. LeRoux, "Companies Aiding Smokers," 64.

10. Ibid.

11. Ibid.

12. Ibid. See also "Higher Premiums Sought for Elderly Smokers," *American Medical News* 28 (February 22, 1986): 10.

13. Brian S. Moskal, "Hup 2-3-4! No Smoking!" *Industry Week* 235 (February 9, 1987): 24-25.

14. Ibid.

15. Braham, "Ban It or Restrict It?," 16.

16. See Maynard Good Stoddard, "The Butt Stops Here," *Saturday Evening Post* 268 (April 1986): 22 for the announcement of the award.

Appendix A: Pacific Northwest Bell
Nonsmoking Policy

BACKGROUND, PACIFIC NORTHWEST BELL, 1983 SURVEY

The issue of smoking and its impact on health is gaining increased attention among employees, and in some work groups, has become the source of disharmony and concern. In order to learn the smoking habits of employees and attitudes toward smokers by non-smokers, Business Research was asked to conduct a baseline employee smoking survey.

OBJECTIVES

The objectives of the employee study were to determine:

• The percentage of smokers in the company.
• The habits and attitudes of smokers versus nonsmokers.
• The level of support for a corporate smoking policy.
• The degree of concern employees have for the current smoking situation in the company.

METHODOLOGY

Questionnaires were mailed to 1,800 employees (occupational and 1st and 2nd level managers), company-wide. The sample was stratified by geographical area, Washington and Oregon, and sampling was done from the Human Resources data base. A total of 1,334 questionnaires were returned for a 74 percent response rate. For this report, the total was weighted so that the results represent the actual employee population.

SUMMARY

Smoking at the Workplace

- 28 percent of the respondents said they regularly smoke.
- 26 percent of the respondents said they smoke cigarettes and 2 percent pipes and cigars.

Attitudes Towards Smoking at the Workplace

- 64 percent of all employees surveyed said that they are at least occasionally bothered by smoking at the workplace.
- 18 percent of smokers said they are at least occasionally bothered by smoke on the job.
- 82 percent of the nonsmokers said they are occasionally bothered by someone else smoking at work.

Reasons for Disliking Smoking in the Workplace

- 52 percent eye irritation
- 51 percent concern for health
- 48 percent makes clothes and hair smell

Perceptions of the Company's Role

- 78 percent of all respondents and 52 percent of all smokers felt that the company should be concerned about smoking at the workplace.
- 77 percent of all respondents and 57 percent of the smokers said they would like some type of smoking policy for their *immediate work area*. The most preferred type of policy (51 percent) was having designated smoking and nonsmoking areas.
- 83 percent of all respondents and 67 percent of the smokers said they would like to have some type of smoking policy for company *training and conference areas*.
- 89 percent of all respondents and 79 percent of the smokers felt thre should be some type of smoking policy for the *cafeteria*.

Smoking and Health

- 45 percent of the nonsmokers rated their overall health as "excellent."
- 31 percent of the smokers rated their overall health as "excellent."

CONCLUSIONS AND IMPLICATIONS

This section of the report is interpretive. Unlike the "Summary" and "Detailed Findings" which report the findings of the Study without comment, this section includes the opinions of [PNB's human resources staff].

Based on the results of this survey, a majority of PNB employees are bothered by smoking at the workplace and are experiencing physical discomfort because of smoking. They feel the company should be concerned about the issue of smoking, mainly because it should be concerned about the health of its employees. A fourth (26%) of the respondents said that smoking interferes with their job performance, which is reason enough for the company to be concerned with smoking at the workplace.

There were strong indications that employees would like to see the company have some type of smoking policy for work areas. Company training and conference areas are a priority with employees for a total ban on smoking. Cafeteria smoking appears to be another source of bother to employees. Either the current policy of designated smoking and nonsmoking areas is not well enough defined or not enforced, because respondents indicated they wanted a policy for the cafeteria.

It has been [PNB's human resources] observation that sometimes employees are skeptical of survey results. They perceive that nothing will change as a result of their input. Correspondingly, in this survey, 151 unsolicited surveys were received, signed by employees giving their opinions on smoking. The message that comes through clearly in both the official and unofficial survey is that employees are concerned about smoking at the workplace and they want the company to respond. The company has an opportunity to assume the responsible role employees consider appropriate and to develop a smoking policy.

The most preferred type of smoking policy by respondents for company work areas was designated smoking and nonsmoking areas. One approach might be to design all the areas based on the number of smokers. For example, since slightly more than ¼ (28%) of the employees smoke, ¼ of the cafeteria would have seating in a smoking section and other ¾ of the cafeteria would be nonsmoking seating. This would correspond to the number of nonsmokers in the company.

PACIFIC NORTHWEST BELL, JULY 15, 1985

Memorandum for All PNB Employees

Over the past 2½ years we have had a Smoking Issues Steering Committee, numerous QWL teams, and ad hoc committees addressing the problems created by smoking in PNB. Many letters, calls and petitions have been received asking that PNB eliminate smoking in the workplace to protect the health of our employees. As a result of this feedback and research, effective October 15, 1985 the PNB Smoking Policy will be:

"To protect the health of PNB employees there will be no smoking in any company facility."

As a former smoker, I realize that this will be difficult for some employees. After examining other companies which have eliminated smoking in the workplace, we've found that the policies are effective and supported by smokers and nonsmokers alike. I'm confident that by working together we can make this the case here at PNB.

The company is not suggesting that employees quit smoking. Smoking is a matter of personal choice. We are only asking that there be no smoking on company premises.

There are a number of reasons why this decision was reached, but the major one is the health issue connected with smoking. A variety of options will be made available to those employees who would like to use the next few months as an opportunity to quit smoking.

As we move toward a smokefree work environment, smokers, ex-smokers and nonsmokers need to work together. Between now and October 15, you'll be receiving more information to ensure that the implementation of the policy is a smooth one. Clean air is important to us all.

L. L. Wolfard
Vice President—Personnel

PACIFIC NORTHWEST BELL, JULY 15, 1985

Smoking Cessation Classes Offered

Today, Larry Wolfard, Vice-President—Personnel, announced a new smoking policy for PNB which eliminates smoking in any company facility effective October 15, 1985.

To assist employees—and their spouses and dependents—who wish to cut down or stop smoking, PNB will pay for the cost of reasonable expenses in connection with completing a smoking cessation program.

A variety of smoking cessation programs are available within and outside PNB. For details on these programs, please call (503) 242-8151 in Oregon and (206) 345-4100 in Washington.

PNB wants to help—please call one of the numbers shown above if you are interested in participating. We'll assist you with class selection and expense information.

Distribution: All PNB Employees

BACKGROUND TO PACIFIC NORTHWEST BELL'S
NO SMOKING POLICY EFFECTIVE OCTOBER 15, 1985

On July 15, 1985 a memorandum was sent to all employees of Pacific Northwest Bell announcing a no-smoking policy. This policy was scheduled to go into effect 90 days later, on October 15, 1985. A copy of this announcement is attached, signed by Larry Wolfard, Vice President of Personnel. The memorandum climaxed two and one-half years of study and investigation by a committee representing most of the primary departments in the company as well as both Unions.

Pacific Northwest Bell's policy is, "To protect the health of PNB employees there will be no smoking in any company facility."

In recent years the company suggestion program has received numerous requests for a no-smoking policy. Letters were also sent to our president, A. V. Smith and other officers of the company, as well as the Health Care Services and Corporate Safety Departments. What had started as an occasional letter soon developed into a strong voice asking to take a stand.

Len Beil, Director of Human Resource Planning and Employee Involvement, who had as part of his job responsibilities emerging issues, formed the committee to look into the smoking issue. Len chaired the group consisting of approximately fifteen employees, representing the Communications Workers of America, the Order of Repeatermen and Toll Testboardmen, Health Care Services, Legal, Public Relations, Personnel, Finance and Comptrollers, Building Operations, and NetCom. Approximately 30 percent of the committee were smokers which is comparable to 28 percent of total PNB employees who smoke. The objective of this committee was to explore alternatives and recommend a policy that was fair and equitable to all employees and consistent with the health and safety message our company promotes.

In May of 1983 a survey was developed and sent to employees. The results of the survey showed that only 28 percent of our employees smoked. Seventy-four percent of the surveys were returned along with 151 additional surveys submitted by employees who wanted to state their opinions.

An overwhelming number of employees, smokers included, wanted a definite policy and felt strongly that both mainstream and sidestream smoke were hazardous to health. After the results of the survey were reviewed by the committee, possible solutions were discussed and implemented. One of the first was that each work group would decide its own policy. This did not work well because it was not viewed by employees as fair and equitable to all employees.

Also, information available to the Committee indicated that there were no current air purifier systems available in the market place capable of removing the gases as well as the particles emitted by cigarette smoke from the air if smoking were permitted in a building. Thus, to provide clean air in a building and allow smoking in a portion of that building, the area where smoking was permitted would have to be vented separately. The Building Operations Department was asked to conduct a feasibility study to determining the cost and practicality of providing separate smoking areas in a sample of thirteen buildings. Pacific Northwest Bell currently has over 750 buildings. The cost averaged between $5,000 and $80,000 per vented room in each building. It was also determined that additions would have to be built onto some of the buildings because of existing space limitations, adding to the impracticality. At that point the unions stated their positions that if smoking were permitted in some buildings it should be allowed in all or none.

Ultimately it was determined that the only viable alternative was to state the current policy and give all our employees the opportunity to work together in a clean air environment.

Mr. Smith and the officers agree with the committee's recommendation and recognizing that this policy would be difficult for some employees to adjust to, agreed to have the Company reimburse employees, their spouse and Class I dependents who chose to attend a smoking cessation program. A "hot line" telephone contact was established in both Washington and Oregon to field calls from employees. The purpose of the hot line was to assist employees in the selection of a cessation program and also to answer questions generated by the announcement of the policy.

Lists of smoking cessation programs available in all PNB areas were developed and each of these were called to verify address and telephone numbers and also to get in-depth information about the program, its specialty, if any, and the cost and possibility of corporate rates for our employees. We found that most programs fell into six primary categories. They are Medical, Aversion therapy, Behavior modificaiton, Acupuncture, Hypnotherapy and Motivational training.

We also recognized that, like diets, different programs work for different people and a commitment to the program is important for success. With that established the employees and their families were free to choose programs that they felt would work for them. Most employees were pleased and surprised that the Company allowed them the choice and that they were not locked into a specific "Company sponsored" program. This seemed to add to their commitment to succeed, and helped to encourage a friendlier attitude toward the policy. Through conversations with the employees we discovered a genuine concern for the budget, spending the money wisely and making it pay off.

An added message that has been reiterated often is that we are not asking the employees to stop smoking, only to refrain from smoking in any Company facility. This, plus the fact that the policy change originated from the employees, not the Officers of the Company, has made the transition period very smooth and relatively quiet. We have received few negative letters and even a form letter, distributed in the cafeteria smoking section of the Corporate headquarters, generated little interest. The primary request received has been to provide at least one smoking area in the building, preferably the cafeteria. At this time time this is not under consideration because of the in-depth study done by the original committee.

Additional information can be obtained by contacting Len Beil in Seattle on (206) 345-2161 or by writing to him at room 2110 Bell Plaza, Seattle, Washington 98191.

PACIFIC NORTHWEST BELL, MAY 15, 1987

When we first started to consider a smoking policy for the workplace at Pacific Northwest Bell we were aware that careful planning and specialized information were the essential components of a successful and effective policy.

During the two and one-half years of research and preparation our Steering Committee consulted with various sources, companies and associations. One of the most helpful in providing expert knowledge, on-site guidance and practical advice were the founders of the Smoking Policy Institute.

We hired Robert Rosner, Executive Director of the Smoking Policy Institute, as a consultant in the spring of 1985 and his advice and direction were invaluable.

Our Pacific Northwest Bell Smoking Policy went into effect October 15, 1985 and has been a complete success.

We are now pleased to be recognized as a model and encouragement to other organizations now addressing the issue of smoking in the work environment.

We receive calls weekly from throughout the country asking for information about our smoking policy. This material hopefully will be of some help to you. If you are looking for additional assistance I recommend contacting the Smoking Policy Institute at 206-324-4444.

Contact: Bruce Amundson   Sept. 24, 1987
          345-6885

BACKGROUND OF PACIFIC NORTHWEST BELL'S "NO SMOKING" POLICY

- By 1983, suggestions from employees that PNB "look into" the smoking issue had increased substantially. In response to that interest, PNB formed a committee to research the issue.

- The joint management and union research committee of 15 employees was formed. The group's objective was to explore alternatives and recommend a smoking policy that was fair and equitable to all employees.

- In May 1983, a survey was mailed to a sample group of employees, asking their opinions on the smoking issue. The survey showed that most employees, including the 28 percent who smoked, wanted a definite policy and felt strongly that both mainstream and sidestream smoke were hazardous to health.

- Several options were discussed including the designation of smoking areas in PNB's 750 facilities. The cost, it soon was realized, was prohibitive. The conclusion was that the only viable course of action was to have PNB employees work in a smoke-free environment. The committee recommended:

"To protect the health of PNB employees, there will be no smoking in any company facility."

- PNB President Andrew Smith and PNB officers agreed with the research committee's recommendation, which included reimbursement for smoking cessation programs for employees, their spouses and dependents.

- Several information programs were begun to help employees learn about cessation programs. A "hot line" was instituted to answer questions employees had about the policy. These were part of an overall program to help those employees who wanted to stop smoking.

• A follow-up questionnaire, geared to determine the "success" of the program, was sent to 1,200 participants in cessation programs reimbursed by PNB. Of the 639 questionnaires returned (53 percent return rate):

—44 percent said they had quit smoking

—30 percent said the program had helped them cut down on smoking

—76 percent said they had tried to quit smoking before

• PNB did not ask employees to stop smoking. Rather, the policy restricts smoking in company facilities.

• PNB will share its very successful "no smoking" plan with other companies that are considering smoke-free workplaces. Additional information can be obtained by writing Len Beil, Director of Human Resource Planning, Bell Plaza, Room 2001, Seattle, WA 98191, or by calling Beil at (206) 345-2161.

Contact: Bruce Amundson   Sept. 24, 1987
        345-6885

SMOKING CESSATION PROGRAMS (AS OF AUGUST 31, 1987)

*	Cessation programs attended	1,738
*	By employees	1,353
*	By spouses	360
*	By dependents	25
*	Types of programs attended	
*	Acupuncture	621
*	Hypnosis	554
*	Behavior modification	437
*	Aversion therapy	54
*	Nicorette gum	51
*	Motivational training	13
*	Vitamin therapy	8

Pacific Northwest Bell pays the cost of cessation programs for its employees, their spouses and dependents. To date, the cost of these programs has been *$247,526.44*, with the average cost being *$142.42*.

PACIFIC NORTHWEST BELL
NEWS RELEASE
SEPTEMBER 24, 1987

CONTACT: Diane du Bois   FOR IMMEDIATE RELEASE
441-5100

Today in Seattle U.S. Surgeon General Dr. C. Everett Koop presented Andy Smith, president, Pacific Northwest Bell, with the American Lung Association of Washington's Corporate Action Award. This award honors outstanding achievements of business leaders who have responded to Dr. Koop's challenge of creating a smokefree society by the year 2000. Dr. Koop praised Mr. Smith for his pioneering work in promoting the smokefree workplace.

Through Mr. Smith's efforts Pacific Northwest Bell, with 15,000 employees at 750 locations in three Northwest states, adopted a no-smoking policy for all company facilities in October of 1985. The action followed more than two years of preparation by Mr. Smith and a steering committee, consisting of company as well as union representatives.

Pacific Northwest Bell is one of the largest companies in the United States to have adopted this type of "complete and total" policy on smoking in the workplace. At Pacific Northwest Bell employees who smoke must leave company buildings to do so. To help them quit the company pays for a variety of smoking cessation programs for employees, spouses and dependents.

Dr. Koop cited the work of Mr. Smith and Pacific Northwest Bell as a model program for the nation.

8

SUGGESTED IMPLEMENTATION
POLICIES AND PROCEDURES:
NEXT STEPS

Implementing a program means getting from where you are (what is) to where you want to be (or, what should be). Thus, implementing a nonsmoking program is changing from the status quo to the program selected by the firm or the agency—typically (as Chapters 6 and 7 showed) a total ban on smoking.

Initially an organization must *identify the problem:* How many smokers work there? What are the attitudes of smokers and nonsmokers, clients, administration, and others? What are the costs of smoking? What are the legal requirements? This stage is identifying values (what should be) and long-range goals, carefully gathering the facts (what is), and measuring the difference (the "gap" or discrepancy). Maximum employee input is desirable.

The second stage is *defining the problem.* Here the organization must identify constraints—cost limitations, building design (say, ventilation system capabilities), union contract provisions, and so forth. But more important the organization must specify a series of measurable objectives (MBOs)—objectives that can be used for subsequent evaluation of mission accomplishment. Measurable objectives will be specific as to who is responsible, by when, how well, how monitored and controlled (reporting requirements), and so on. Employee input is critical.

Step three is *analyzing the problem*—methodically taking the problem (nonsmoking policy and program) apart and being certain the organization understands all the ramifications of the issue (hiring policies, smoking cessation progams, news releases, how to best sign entrances and facilities as nonsmoking areas, grievance procedure and discipline policies). Employee input is critical to be sure the problem is thoroughly analyzed—torn apart, studied, reviewed.

Step four is *generating alternative solutions.* Once the nonsmoking issue has been identified, defined, and analyzed, the organization should seek solutions from some or all of these sources—reviews of the literature, expert opinion, visits to successful programs elsewhere, pilot programs (experimenting at one location for a year before gong companywide), brainstorming, and so on. Maximum input from employees is more than desirable: Anyone may offer an idea or a solution that others would not have considered. The authors urge that organizations seeking solutions (alternatives) strive for quantity, not quality—that is, anything goes at this stage—just possible solutions that can be conceptualized as alternative strategies to solving the problem.

- Use a heterogeneous team. Mix the brainstorming team members up (newcomers, old timers; blue collar, pink collar; young, old; etc.) to avoid "group think" and stereotypical ideas.

- Strive for quantity, not quality. Anything goes, any idea should be raised. Determination of the merits of each idea is saved for later. Set goals of "30 ideas" or "50 ideas" and see how quickly the group can exceed those numbers. Any idea should be listed.

- Defer judgment. Don't let team members critique or criticize proposed solutions. The team leader must prevent anyone from evaluating ideas—the creative juices dry up quickly when the team bogs down into discussion of ideas. Don't allow this—keep the process moving along so the number of ideas is greatly increased.

- Incubate. Wherever possible let the team think about the problem subconciously— over a weekend, overnight, over a lunch period, as long as possible. Evidence suggests the best ideas emerge after a period of incubation. The human brain has a remarkable facility to solve complex problems after a period of quiet contemplation or meditation.

Too many teams violate the spirit and the letter of every one of these four substeps. Applying them results in rich dividends. After generating many ideas (from a variety of sources) the team (or a few designated team members) should "refine the ideas into solution strategies." That is, reduce the many ideas to a few broader strategies. Almost always 30-50-70 ideas reduce themselves (by bunching or chaining related ideas together) to 5-7-9 mutually exclusive alternative strategies (that is, competitor strategies that are "stand alone" or will solve the problem by themselves). This substep alone typically generates the best and brightest of ideas. This handful of strategies is now ready for vigorous comparison.

Step five is *selecting the best solution or strategy.* Some call this stage cost/benefit analysis. Whatever, here each alternative strategy from step four is subjected to rigorous comparison one by one and with each other: What are the advantages? The disadvantages? The real costs? The benefits (usually estimated)? Employee input is vital in measuring costs and benefits and in the process of comparison. Here the organization eliminates all options but the strategy best designed to achieve all objectives.

Step six is *implementing the strategy selected.* Fundamentally, this is the detailed plan for getting the organization from what is to what ought to be—for closing the gap. The plan provides the step-by-step detail of who, when, what, where, how, and so on. It may be brief or lengthy, written or flowcharted. What is vital is that it communicates a sense of mission, a clear strategy, furnishes precise objectives, and so on. Obviously, employee input is critical: A sense of commitment and ownership is created and provided for. Good plans may not be perfect (no one anticipates everything) but they spell out all levels of responsibility, authority, and involvement.

Step seven is *evaluating and revising.* Real life suggests nothing ever turns out exactly as planned for. (Who could have predicted the freak windstorm that upset the best planned June wedding that ever was?) So, in implementing a nonsmoking program, every organization must periodically evaluate or take stock of where they are and how things are going and then make necessary revisions and adjustments. Clearly, employee input is vital in evaluating program progress (or lack of it) and making the necessary changes. Changes must be clearly communicated to everyone involved in the initial planning and implementation.

Many of the antismoking groups around the country have done extensive research on how organizations can carry out these seven steps. Some models are particularly useful in the authors' judgment. For instance, let us begin with the American Lung Association's model.

The American Lung Association urged that government agencies and corporations "put it in writing" and recommends organizations "draw up a formal written smoking policy"; but the Association recommends keeping it simple yet specific.[1] The Lung Association has model policies from giant corporations as well as small businesses that they will furnish as examples. Further, the Lung Association suggests scheduling "appropriate middle-management meetings to review the policy and to stress its importance," and that organizations "inform employees that the smoking policy has the solid backing of top management and, if appropriate, union leadership." They suggest that "a letter from the President or Chief Executive Officer to each employee is one way to convey management support." Lastly, the Lung Association encourages sending "every employee a copy of the new policy before the effective date. Also, direct supervisors to go over the policy with employees at staff meetings so any questions or problems can be resolved in advance."

The Lung Association suggests that organizations recognize nonsmoking as the norm. Indeed, they say,

The central concept in new company policies—and the basis of many new laws in states, cities, counties, and town governing workplace smoking—is this principle: the preferences of nonsmokers and smokers will be addressed and accommodated, whenever possible. However, when these preferences conflict, the rights and preferences of the nonsmoker will prevail. Whether or not there is a law or ordinance yet in your community, you can make this concept central to your company's policy.

The Lung Association says that "companies with the most effective, harmonious policies have adopted these approaches":

- Before an organization considers direct action, it may wish to conduct a survey to determine employees' attitudes throughout the company or agency and to encourage employee suggestions.

- Once the organization decides to proceed, it should pledge the solid support of top management and enlist the cooperation of all levels of management. The assistance of supervisors (particularly first-level supervisors) will be essential to promoting positive employee attitudes toward the new policy and in practical matters such as internal communication and policy enforcement, when necessary.

- The organization should request the input and assistance of all employees in formulating the policy. This can best be done, the Lung Association feels, by scheduling discussions at staff meetings and forming an employee committee (with smokers and nonsmokers on the committee) to advise on the design of the policy.

- The organization should emphasize at every opportunity its concern for the health of its employees, nonsmokers and smokers alike, and that its concern is the crucial reason for implementing a smoking policy (not cost reduction, for instance).

- The Lung Association recognizes some employees may accuse the organization of "changing the rules." In response, management should stress that the organization is developing a smoking policy because new information has come to light about smoking at the workplace. Management should point out that over the years it has made many other rule changes, such as increased benefits, that have been readily accepted by most employees.

The American Cancer Society urges a model policy as follows:[2]

Policy

It is the policy of (Name of Company) to respect the rights of both the nonsmoker and the smoker in Company buildings and facilities.

When these rights conflict, management and (Name of Company) employees should endeavor to find a reasonable accommodation. When such an accommodation is not possible, the rights of the nonsmoker should prevail.

Smoking is always not permitted in areas where there is sensitive or hazardous material and in other places designated by the Company.

Prohibited Areas

Smoking is not permitted in areas with sensitive equipment, computer systems, or where records and supplies would be exposed to hazard from fires, ashes or smoke.

Smoking is prohibited where combustible fumes can collect such as in garage and storage areas, areas where chemicals are used and all other designated areas where an occupational safety or health hazard might exist.[3]

Smoking is not permitted in confined areas of general access such as: libraries, medical facilities, cashier waiting lines, elevators, restrooms, stairwells, copy rooms, lobbies, waiting rooms and fitness centers.

Smoking is not permitted where Company premises are frequently visited by customers, such as public offices and customer service areas.

The Company may designate other locations where smoking is not permitted.

Work Areas

In work areas, where space is shared by two or more persons, an effort shall be made to accommodate individual preferences to the degree prudently possible. When requested, managers shall make a reasonable attempt to separate persons who smoke from those who do not.

Employees may designate their private offices as smoking or nonsmoking areas. Visitors to private work areas should honor the wishes of the host.

In Company vehicles, including Company-sponsored van pools, smoking shall be permitted only when there is no objection from one or more of the occupants.

Areas of Common Use

In meetings and enclosed locations, such as conference rooms and classrooms, smoking will not be permitted. Breaks and appropriate access to public areas may be scheduled to accommodate the needs of smokers.

In enclosed locations of common use, such as cafeterias, dining areas, employee lounges, and auditoriums, smoking shall be permitted only in identified smoking sections, providing there is adequate ventilation and they are not normal customer areas. Smoking is permitted in corridors.

Employees and visitors are expected to honor the smoking and nonsmoking designations and to be considerate of nonsmokers in their vicinity.

Personnel Manual

The smoking policy most likely would be placed in a personnel manual or employee handbook to facilitate its distribution to employees.

Employees should be encouraged to discuss any concerns with their manager. Since this is not always practical, complaint or grievance procedures should be included in the manual/handbook. Such complaints might involve either a medical or an employee relations referral.

Enforcement of the policy is most equitable when placed as a responsibility on all employees. Other alternatives are to specify managers/supervisors or other appropriate individuals as responsible for enforcement.

Education and Training

To further enhance the above policy, employees who smoke should be offered information about the dangers involved in smoking and offered opportunities to change to a nonsmoking lifestyle.

Smokers seeking assistance should be offered it on a regular basis. Educational and cessation programs can usually be arranged by the Company's Medical, Personnel or Training Department. Low-cost programs are often available from several community organizations. Each Company or division is responsible for determining the budget for this program, whether it will be conducted by Company health professionals or outside organizations, and whether the course will be offered during or outside normal working hours.

The Cancer Society recognizes the potential issue of occupational exposure (for instance, see related case materials in Chapter 6). Therefore, the Cancer Society urges that all smoking policies of an organization should also address the issue of occupational exposure and smoking where the combined effect of both is known to be hazardous to employee health. In such cases, the Cancer Society says, the supporting evidence for restricting smoking is clear. An additional and growing concern on the part of many is the effect of sidestream or passive smoke. The Cancer Society acknowledges that, "while there is still debate as to the exact physical effects on the individual, the matter is increasingly being considered." The Society feels some newer policies, thrrefore, "also restrict smoking in work environments where it may be a social irritant and/or associated with a medical problem."

One very partisan group, GASP of New York, Inc. (Group Against Smoking Pollution) has suggested a "plan of action for employees" who want their organization to become a nonsmoking place of employment.[4] GASP urges employees to use any or all of the following avenues in making their workplace smokefree. Employees should contact their Health, Labor, and Fire Departments to find out if any nonsmoking laws apply to their workplace. If they do, employees should see that they are enforced.

Employees should poll others in their workplace. They may find that many are also adversely affected by secondhand smoke and will work with nonsmokers. Employees should distribute a petition seeking support for a nosmoking policy and present petitions to management.

Workers should be diplomatic about nonsmoking and always present their case in a reasonable and calm manner. They should speak to their superiors emphasizing secondhand smoke's health hazards and their genuine concern at being subjected to harmful substances as part of their job. Workers should tell them they are only requesting a healthy work environment. Nonsmokers should have a chat with smoking coworkers and tell them, "I recognize your need to smoke, but we all share the same air and I am genuinely concerned about my health." They may receive immediate consideration. A fair solution, in which the needs of both smokers and nonsmokers are met, can be achieved with reasonable dialogue and cooperation by management, smokers, and nonsmokers, GASP finds. However, if reasonable dialogue fails, workers should send a memo to their superiors (immediate and higher), the medical officer, union representative, health and safety committee, and top boss. They should include a copy of their personal physician's note if secondhand smoke has been determined the cause of an employee's ailment. Workers should request a meeting to discuss the problem and to seek an agreeable solution.

Nonsmokers should keep a diary and document all the action they take, their physical problems, their visits to their personal physician and/or to their company medical department, number of hours per week they are exposed to secondhand smoke, physical layout of their workplace, type of ventilation, and management's response or lack of it. Workers should retain copies of all memos and correspondence. They will need this documentation in case they decide to apply for unemployment insurance, retire on disability, be treated as a handicapped person, or take legal action, GASP suggests. "Legal precedents have been established in litigation and workers' compensation claims which have been settled in favor of the nonsmoker's right to work in a safe and wholesome environment and not to have to inhale cancer-inducing pollutants during performance of duties," says GASP.

Employees should continue to document their nonsmoking concerns. If management offers to try certain plans, workers should document the implementation and effectiveness of such plans. GASP suggests that management may try to placate nonsmokers by offering worthless solutions such as "(a) having smokers and nonsmokers sit at different ends of the same conference table; (b) placing smokers near a barely open window; (c) placing a table top filter on a desk; (d) offering other worthless token plans to humor them in the hope that nonsmokers will pursue it no further." GASP says nonsmokers should not accept any plan that is not satisfactory to them and explore all channels, as high in management as necessary, to "clear the air at work."

Last, workers should write to their health commissioners and legislators at all levels of government and request smoking restriction legislation to cover *all* workplaces, regardless of size, area, or number of employees, says GASP. They should request legislation similar to San Francisco's amendment to the health code, which rules that "if an accommodation which is satisfactory to all nonsmoking employees cannot be reached in *any* given workplace, the preferences of nonsmoking employees should prevail in that office workplace." San Francisco's Health Department reports very little difficulty in enforcing this ruling.

Clearly, management may find some of GASP's recommendations as offensive, even counterproductive. Still, taken as a whole, it is a logically thought-through plan of action.

GASP has also suggested a few additional steps on implementation of a no-smoking policy that may have merit:

- Offer incentives for kicking the habit such as (a) bring a smoking cessation program into the workplace during lunch, after work, or allow work release time for attending; (b) pay for an outside smoking cessation program; (c) offer a bonus for quitting smoking.

- If there is a drug and alcohol program, add tobacco.

- Remove ashtrays in all no-smoking areas. Ashtrays are an invitation to smoke. Place butt receptacles outside entrances to no-smoking areas.

- Remove cigarette machines. Replace with fresh fruit or juice machines.

- Electrostatic precipitators and ion generators do not clear out the harmful gases in tobacco smoke, but may clear some of the particulates. These devices will not clear the air for nonsmokers, but may help reduce the *smokers'* risk if placed in a *separate smoking area*. Tabletop filters and smokeless ashtrays help very little. Banning smoking in work areas is the best solution.

Appendix A to this chapter provides a number of examples of company nonsmoking policies and programs by states and regions. It was provided by the Office of Disease Prevention and Health Promotion, U.S. Department of Health and Human Services, Washington, D.C. Updated versions are issued periodically.

The American Cancer Society, American Heart Association, and American Lung Association cosponsored a report for the U.S. Department of Health and Human Services called *No Smoking: A Decision Maker's Guide to Reducing Smoking at the Worksite.*[5] This guide suggests that "in addition to the voluntary agencies and government offices listed below, some trade organizations, especially those representing health or insurance groups, and a growing number of not-for-profit firms also provide materials that may be of special interest to employers wishing to limit smoking." The Public Health Service then describes these seven free resources as follows.

American Cancer Society. The American Cancer Society (ACS) offers a full array of smoking control services to business and industry. These range from providing pamphlets, posters, envelope stuffers, ads, newsletter articles, and other informational items on smoking, to offering self-help materials that will aid smokers who wish to quit on their own, to presenting in-house small-group cessation clinics. The Society will provide speakers and audiovisual materials for programs on the hazards of smoking and benefits of quitting and trained facilitators to conduct in-house "FreshStart" cessation groups. The ACS will also train and support employees who are ex-smokers and who are interested in facilitating the company's own ongoing group cessation program. Finally, the Society will help plan a program that is tailored to the overall needs of both employer and employee, as well as provide materials to aid in formulating a company smoking policy.

To find out more about ACS smoking control services and materials and to arrange an appointment with an ACS representative, contact your local American Cancer Society.

American Heart Association. The American Heart Association is a nonprofit voluntary health organization dedicated solely to the reduction of premature death and disability from heart and blood vessel diseases. The Association works toward this goal through programs in research, public education, professional education, and community service. While the services provided by AHA's many affiliates vary, local heart associations can assist worksites in establishing smoking policies and in developing and implementing self-help smoking cessation programs. Local AHAs offer a range of publications and also may be able to offer guidelines for developing worksite programs in high blood pressure control and nutrition education. For further information about these and other programs and services, get in touch with your local American Heart Association.

American Lung Association. There are more than 140 Lung Associations around this country, and all have materials to help companies reduce smoking among employees. While the materials available and services offered vary from location to location, many can supply the "Freedom from Smoking" self-help manual for those who wish to quit on their own (IBM has distributed 30,000 sets at company expense to employees who requested them), as well as conduct the "Freedom from Smoking" clinics, both of which have been tested nationally. Lung Associations also have expertise and tools to assist organizations in developing smoking policies. Two new publications focus on the importance of developing policies to restrict smoking, one aimed at influencing top management to take action and the other designed to provide how-to information. To learn about these and other services and materials that may be available, contact your local American Lung Association.

Office on Smoking and Health. The Office's Technical Information Center serves as a central and accessible source of scientific and technical information about smoking. In addition to developing the annual *Surgeon General's Report on Smoking*, the Office on Smoking and Health has thousands of articles on smoking in its data bank, and it offers a bimonthly publication, *Smoking and Health Bulletin*, that contains abstracts of current smoking literature in seventeen categories. Its Public Information Office also provides consumer-oriented information. A free booklet, "The Technical Information Center," describes the publications and services of the office. To obtain material or request information, write to the Office on Smoking and Health, Park Building, Room 1-10, 5600 Fishers Lane, Rockville, Md. 20857.

National Cancer Institute. The Office of Cancer Communications within the National Cancer Institute has undertaken a major cancer education effort. Although some materials, like the twenty-page booklet *Good News: Better News: Best News,* focus on cancer in general rather than smoking specifically, they still could be used effectively as part of a worksite program. A new "Quit for Good" kit has been designed for use especially by physicians, dentists, and pharmacists, which could be useful to worksite occupational physicians or to local private practice care givers. Each kit contains enough material for use with fifty patients or clients. Since most people have a great respect for the health advice provided by physicians, dentists, and pharmacists, these kits could supplement worksite programs. To receive a copy of the kit and other materials, or to get assistance in starting a cancer awareness program, contact the Office of Cancer Communications, National Cancer Institute, Building 31, Room 10A18, Bethesda, Md. 20205.

National Health Information Clearinghouse (NHIC). This free service of the Office of Disease Prevention and Health Promotion offers one-stop shopping for information on smoking and other topics. NHIC will take your request and direct it to several appropriate organizations that will, in turn, provide you with the information on smoking or any health-related topic. Contact the Clearinghouse if you want information but do not know where to turn. Call the NHIC toll-free number, 800-336-4797 (in Virginia 703-522-5290) or write to P.O. Box 1133, Washington, D.C. 20013-1133.

National Heart, Lung, and Blood Institute (NHLBI). The NHLBI offers several resources that may be useful in a worksite smoking cessation program. A series of seven video vignettes and a leader's guide are available for purchase. Titled "We Can't Go on Like This," this package can be used to stimulate discussion about why people smoke, to expose obstacles to quitting, and to motivate smokers to quit. Contact the National Audiovisual Center, Information Services MD, Washington, D.C. 20409. Several fact sheets, suitable for reproduction and covering topics like smoking and your heart, as well as a publication designed specifically for physicians, "How to Help Your Hypertensive Patients Stop Smoking," are available from NHLBI. For these and other materials, contact NHLBI, Public Inquiries and Reports Branch, NIH, Room 4A21, Bethesda, Md. 20205.

Weis and Wick have written that "health care resource managers should not view smoking control as merely an inevitable step to ward off the demons of disease, disability, death, and litigation."[6] Rather, they say, "smoking control can and should be viewed as a positive step toward creating a more desirable and productive work environment, and toward developing a more favorable image among current and prospective clients."

The same writers, having studied and worked with organizations that have instituted many different types of nonsmoking policies, have found that the bottom line in all cases—no matter what the cost—is a mere fraction of the financial benefits. Weis and Wick say some organizations have developed and implemented bans at virtually no cost whatsoever. For example, Boyd Coffee in Portland, Oregon, instituted its smoking policy by posting a notice on a Friday announcing that smoking would no longer be allowed, effective the next Monday. Weis and Wick added, "there was the obligatory binding arbitration, but that was a mere inconvenience and concession to form. Costs to the company were negligible."

At the other end of the spectrum, they suggest, organizations such as Group Health Cooperative hired independent consultants to plan and direct the phase-in period of nonsmoking programs. But even at this high end of the investment spectrum, Weis and Wick write, the costs were recaptured within months of the program's inception. Moreover, they concluded that many companies found that the long-term approach was helpful in winning strong employee support for the program. They concluded that, "if cessation incentives are offered to smokers as part of the smoke-free program, then a conservative estimate by [Weis and Wick] for costs might run in the $200 to $350 range for every smoker on the payroll, inclusive of costs for policy design, phase-in, incentives and enforcement (assuming an organization with at least 100 smokers)." These are conservative estimates in this author's opinion.

Finally, the American Lung Association in *Creating Your Company Policy: Freedom from Smoking at Work* has suggested the following "Employee Survey About Smoking at Work," as part of successfully involving workers and implementing a program that works.[7]

1. **What is your opinion of a smoking policy for your immediate work area?**
   (Check one)

   There should be no restrictions   ____1

   There should be a total ban on
   smoking   ____2

   There should be designated
   smoking & nonsmoking areas   ____3

   Other (please specify)   ____4

2. What is your opinion of a smoking policy for <u>other areas</u> at the workplace?
   (Check appropriate column at right)

	1 There should be no restrictions	2 There should be a total ban on smoking	3 There should be designated smoking & non- smoking areas
a) conference room	_____	_____	_____
b) cafeteria	_____	_____	_____
c) breakroom (lounge)	_____	_____	_____
d) elevators	_____	_____	_____
e) restrooms	_____	_____	_____
f) other (please specify)	_____	_____	_____

3. Do you feel our company should offer   Yes   ____1
   programs to employees to help them   No   ____2
   stop smoking?

4. Please indicate the extent to which   Frequently   ____1
   you are bothered by someone else   Occasionally   ____2
   smoking at work.   Seldom   ____3
      Never   ____4

5. If you are bothered by smoking at work,   Clothes & hair smell   ____1
   in what way are you bothered?   Eye irritation   ____2
   (select all that apply)   Coughing   ____3
      Headaches   ____4
      Interferes with work
   Other (please describe) _____   performance   ____5
      Concern for long-term
   _____   health effects   ____6

6. How would you classify your current   Current cigarette smoker   ____1
    smoking status?   Current pipe or cigar
                                                    smoker   ____2
                                                Ex-smoker   ____3
                                                Never smoked   ____4

The Following Two Questions Are To Be Answered By
Current Cigarette Smokers Only

7. If our company offered a program to   Yes   ____1
    help you stop smoking, would you attend?   No   ____2
                                                Not sure   ____3

8. If our company introduced a policy which   It would not affect my
    restricted smoking on company premises,   smoking   ____1
    how do you think this would affect your   I would probably smoke
    overall smoking?   more away from work   ____2
    (select only one)   It might reduce the
                                                    overall amount I smoke   ____3
                                                I might try to quit   ____4

Optional
The Following Questions Should Be Answered By All Employees

9. How many employees are there in your   1-5   ____1
    immediate work area?   6-10   ____2
                                                11-50   ____3

109

10. How many employees in your immediate   None   ____1

     work area smoke cigarettes?   1-5   ____2

                                             6-10   ____3

                                             11-50   ____4

11. Are you . . .   Male   ____1

                                       Female   ____2

12. What is your age?   18-25   ____1

                                       26-35   ____2

                                       36-55   ____3

                                       Over 55   ____4

13. Are you . . . Management   ____1   Non-Management   ____2

14. Additional Comments: _____

_____

_____

The Lung Association also provides three versions of nonsmoking policies. Version 1 is easy to implement but hard to administer. Ultimately it provides little protection for employees or the organization. It basically calls for efforts at satisfactory compromise and promotes goodwill between smokers and nonsmokers.

The Lung Association's nonsmoking policy, version 2, clearly sets forth the organization's proposed nonsmoking policy but still allows smoking in work areas where smokers and nonsmokers work together—even though smoking is specifically prohibited in most designated work areas.

Version 3 prohibits smoking throughout the organization's premises but sets aside some smoking areas if requested by workers. This author is reminded of Weis and Wick's conclusion that tolerating smoking at all can damage the corporate image, especially in organizations related in any way to health care.[8] They describe one specific example.

In Seattle, where hospitals are plentiful and patients scarce, one hospital grabbed the competitive edge by boldly proclaiming itself a "smokefree hospital." Within two months, nearly every hospital in the city had erected similar signs on every entryway. When the supply of services is strong and the demand weak, no hospital can afford to distinguish itself as the one that does not take the health business seriously.

The Lung Association's preferred policy version is simple: it "prohibits smoking throughout company facilities, starting on January 1, 198x."

We conclude this chapter with a lengthy plan of action also proposed by the Lung Association. The authors have reviewed many proposed next steps to implementing an organization's nonsmoking policy—several of these are cited in this chapter. We have not seen a better action plan than ALA's, however, as follows:

Initial Planning

—Assign overall responsibility for developing the policy to a single individual, preferably a member of senior or middle management.

—Set a time line for developing and implementing the smoking policy.

—Appoint an advisory committee composed of managers, union representatives, and staff employees (smokers and nonsmokers) who will assist the lead person in developing recommendations.

—Hold an advisory committee meeting to:

* Review American Lung Association material on smoking policies, secondhand smoke, smoking cessation, and so on.

* Discuss company characteristics that will affect smoking policy content and format.

* Plan how to obtain employee input (formal survey, discussions at staff meetings).

* Request suggested questions for employee survey and/or topics for discussion at staff meetings.

Employee Survey

—Prepare employee survey and/or discussion guidelines.

—Inform all employees of the company's plan to establish a smoking policy.

—Distribute employee survey and/or instruct all supervisors to hold discussions according to guidelines.

—Compile results of employee survey or discussions.

Policy Preparation

—Hold an advisory committee meeting to:

* Review employee input.

- Discuss in detail the specific content and format of the smoking policy.

—Prepare draft of smoking policy based on the input of top management, the advisory committee, union leadership, and employees.

—Distribute copies of policy draft to advisory committee members for their review prior to next meeting.

—Hold an advisory committee meeting to:

- Review, revise, and finalize the smoking policy.

- Discuss the types of "no smoking" and "smoking permitted" signs to be used and their locations.

—Decide how to inform employees about the policy well in advance of its effective date. One or more of the following options should be considered:

- Personal letter from top management to each employee, along with a copy of the policy.

- Announcements at staff meetings.

- Articles about the policy in company and union newsletters.

- Posting of policy on bulletin boards.

- Series of notices in payroll envelopes reminding employees about the policy as the effective date approaches.

Communications Program

—Prepare communications schedule for conveying information on the policy to employees.

—Initiate and assign preparation of communications for employees.

—Order appropriate signs. (Attractive wall and desk-top signs can be obtained free of charge from the American Lung Association, or you may wish to print your own.)

—Hold an advisory committee meeting to:

- Review employee communications schedule.

- Discuss policy enforcement, including the need to provide supervisors with guidelines regarding enforcement procedures.

- Determine the need for an employee awareness program and/or smoking cessation programs. Consult your Lung Association.

—Complete preparation of communications for employees.

—Begin program of employee communications.

Policy Information

—Inform supervisors what will be expected of them in terms of policy enforcement.

—Make arrangements for posting signs and making desk-top signs available to employees.

—Complete program of employee communications with final reminder that smoking policy takes effect on _____, 19__.

—Distribute and post "no smoking" signs the evening before the policy takes effect.

—Begin consistent enforcement of smoking policy on effective date.

Sometime later you may want to assess progress and review the policy. You can conduct a new survey and examine employee input. Your initial policy should evolve as conditions change and information is collected. You may reconvene meetings of your advisory committee on a semiyearly basis.

SUMMARY

In the last few years, a heated controversy has arisen over secondhand smoke (or sidestream smoke) in the workplace and the costs of smoking versus nonsmoking among employees. The American Tobacco Institute and other pro-smoking groups have waged a carefully modulated campaign for some years now, appealing to reason and goodwill in resolving disagreements between smokers and nonsmokers. This campaign has been countered by clean indoor air acts passed or strengthened by some thirty-six states and by aggressive and sometimes strident campaigns by nonsmoker rights' groups.[9] Many public agencies and private firms have begun studying the smoking/ nonsmoking issue or have taken various other steps of action.

This chapter has reviewed these next steps and suggested action plans, as well as defined model policies for organizations considering a nonsmoking policy.

NOTES

1. American Lung Association, *Creating Your Company Policy: Freedom from Smoking at Work* (1985). The seven steps above are adapted from William M. Timmins, "Designing the Q-C Agenda: Next Steps," *Quality Digest* 8 (December 1988): 79-82.

2. American Cancer Society, *Model Policy for Smoking in the Workplace* (n.d.).

3. See the material by the National Safety Council on this subject in "Fire Safety," *Supervisors Safety Manual* (Chicago: National Safety Council, 1985): 387-416.

4. Rhoda Nichter, *Guide to a Smoke-free Workplace* (New York: Group Against Smoking Pollution, n.d.).

5. U.S. Public Health Service, op. cit., pp. 39-41. See also Michael Kunze and Michael Wood, eds., *Guidelines on Smoking Cessation* (Geneva: International Union Against Cancer, 1984) for suggestions on motivating workers to stop on their own, mass media campaigns, self-instruction literature, psychological aspects of cessation, a pharmacological approach to cessation, and so forth. Also see Richard J. Coelho, *Quitting Smoking: A Psychological Experiment Using Community Research* (New York:

Peter Lang, 1985) for considerable detail on sampling methodologies, surveys and questionnaires, and a description of a number of cessation techniques.

6. William L. Weis and Nancy Wick, "Increasing Productivity through On-site Smoking Control," *Health Care Strategic Management* (April 1985): 16-19. The footnotes to Weis and Wick offer some excellent source materials. Weis and Miller also suggest a "Model Timetable for Change," a series of attitude surveys, checklists, and so on. William L. Weis and Bruce W. Miller, *The Smoke-free Workplace* (Buffalo: Prometheus Books, 1985). Lawrence Z. Lorber and J. Robert Kirk, *Fear Itself . . .* (Alexandria, Va.: ASPA Foundation, 1987) in Chapter 5, "Smoking in the Workplace": 35-41 has a brief but useful section called "A Measured Approach to Smoking."

7. American Lung Association, *Creating Your Company Policy.*

8. Weis and Wick, "Increasing Productivity": 19.

9. William M. Timmins, "States Legislate Indoor Clean Air Acts," *Public Administration Times* 9 (February 15, 1986):3.

Appendix A: Nonsmoking Policies and Programs by States and Regions

D.C./MARYLAND/VIRGINIA

- Center for Science in the Public Interest
  Washington, D.C.
  Contact: Michael F. Jacobson
  (202) 332-9110
  Smoking banned in the workplace.

- Clark Enterprises
  Bethesda, Md.
  Contact: Kendra Smith
  (301) 657-7100
  Smoking is banned from the building except in the lobby.

- Oracle Corporation
  Bethesda, Md.
  Contact: Dianne Siegel
  (301) 951-9190
  Smoking is banned in the workplace.

- General Health, Inc.
  Washington, D.C.
  Contact: Hilda Cashman
  (202) 965-4881
  Smoking is banned in the workplace.

- Washington Business Group on Health
  Washington, D.C.
  Contact: Ruth Behrens
  (202) 547-6644

Smoking is banned in the workplace. Only nonsmokers are hired.

ARIZONA/CALIFORNIA/COLORADO/SOUTH DAKOTA/OREGON/WASHINGTON

- Merle Norman Cosmetics
  Los Angeles, Calif.
  (213) 641-3000
  Smoking is banned except in specially ventilated areas of the cafeteria.
- Pacific Telesis
  San Francisco, Calif.
  Contact: Michael Erickson
  (415) 542-9814
  Smoking is restricted to certain areas. The policy is designed to accommodate the preference of both nonsmokers and smokers to the greatest extent possible. Smoking is allowed only where it does not endanger life or property or cause discomfort or unreasonable annoyance to other employees.
- Speedcall Corporation
  Haywood, Calif.
  (415) 279-6565
  Smoking is banned except in restrooms and small designated areas in the lunchroom. Program director sponsors smoking cessation courses, and company reimburses part of the registration fee to those who successfully quit.
- Austad Company
  Sioux Falls, S.D.
  Contact: Oscar Austad, president
  (605) 336-3135
  People from all over the country contact Austad for employment because it has offered a smokefree environment since it was established in 1963.
- Group Health Cooperative of Puget Sound
  Seattle, Wash.
  Contact: Neal S. Sofian
  (206) 326-7100
  Smoking is prohibited in all GHC's twenty clinics, its administrative facilities, and in all its hospitals (except one where smoking is permitted in one area from 7 p.m. to 6 a.m.).
- Northern Life Insurance Company
  Seattle, Wash.
  Contact: Leah Woodruff
  (206) 292-1111 x 493
  Smoking is restricted to designated areas. Company now hires only nonsmokers. Incentives to those who quit include 50 percent reimbursement for cessation pro-

grams and a $200 bonus to those who stop smoking and remain a nonsmoker for one year.

- Pacific Northwest Bell
  Seattle, Wash.
  Contact: Bruce Admundson
  (206) 345-6885
  Beginning October 15, 1985, smoking was prohibited at the workplace.

- Pro-tec
  Bellevue, Wash.
  Contact: Dennis Burns, president
  (206) 828-6595
  No smoking is allowed anywhere in the building or on the grounds. Beginning in 1975, the company hired only nonsmokers.

- Kentrox Industries
  Portland, Oreg.
  Contact: Glenna Kruger
  (503) 643-1681
  Smoking is banned with the exception of half of the lunchroom.

- Radar Electric
  Washington and Oregon
  Contact: Adie Spencer, office manager
  (206) 282-2511
  Neither employees nor customers have been allowed to smoke in Radar Electric's three stores since 1977. Smoking employees are encouraged to stop through a 50 percent rebate on cessation programs.

CONNECTICUT/MASSACHUSETTS/NEW JERSEY/ NEW YORK/PENNSYLVANIA

- Johnson and Johnson
  New Brunswick, N.J.
  Contact: Curtis Wilbur, Ph.D.
  (201) 524-6111
  Smoking is restricted to designated areas; smoking cessation programs are offered.

- Campbell Soup Company
  Camden, N.J.
  Contact: Roland Wear, M.D., medical director
  (609) 964-4000
  On-site smoking cessation courses are offered; tuition reimbursement or subsidies are given for community programs.

- Rodale Press
  Emmaus, Penn.
  Contact: Robert Rodale, president
  (215) 967-5171
  Smoking is banned completely; the company subsidizes participation in smoking cessation classes and issues bonuses to those who successfully quit.
- Provident Indemnity Life Insurance Company
  Norristown, Penn.
  Contact: Maryann Fichter
  (215) 279-2500
  Smoking is banned completely from the workplace. Smokers pay in the vicinity of $300 per year more for insurance coverage than nonsmokers.
- Stanley Works
  New Britain, Conn.
  Contact: Tom Kempa
  (203) 827-3827
  Smoking is restricted to designated areas only. The company offers smoking cessation programs and a partial rebate for those who successfully complete the program.

ILLINOIS/INDIANA/IOWA/KANSAS/ARKANSAS/ KENTUCKY/MICHIGAN/MINNESOTA/MISSOURI/ NEBRASKA/OHIO/WISCONSIN/TENNESSEE

- Bonne Bell
  Lakewood, Ohio
  Contact: Connie Schaffer
  (216) 221-0800
  Smoking is banned in the offices. Employees may smoke only in a smoking room and then only at specific breaks for fifteen minutes. Employees who quit smoking for at least six months are given $250. However, if within the year smoking is resumed, the employee must pay back $500, which is given to a local charity.
- Mahoning Culvert Division of Youngstown Steel Steel and Alloy Corporation
  Canfield, Ohio
  Contact: Warren Freed, president
  (216) 533-5563
  Smokers who quit contribute $.50 per day into a pool for a year-end total of $182.50. At the end of the year, the company adds $817.50 to reward those who are still not smoking with $1,000. The second year, the contributions total $500.
- General Motors Corporation, New Center Area
  Detroit, Mich.
  Contact: Judi Gualtieri
  (313) 556-5000

GM subsidizes 75 percent of the registration fee for employees' participation in a smoking cessation program.

- Park-Nicollet Medical Clinic
  St. Louis Park, Minn.
  Contact: Maureen McCullough
  (612) 927-3123
  Smoking is restricted to designated areas.

- Honeywell, Inc.
  Minneapolis, Minn.
  Contact: Steve Roberts
  (612) 870-2175
  Smoking is restricted to designated areas.

- Scherer Brothers Lumber Company
  Minneapolis, Minn.
  Contact: Bob Peters
  (612) 379-9633
  Smoking is restricted to designated areas.

- MSI Insurance
  Arden Hill, Minn.
  Contact: Gordon Lindquist, CEO
  (612) 631-7000
  Smoking is banned in the workplace. The company assists employees through smoking cessation programs, subsidies for programs taken in the community, educational materials, and contests.

- Hubbard Milling
  Mankato, Minn.
  Contact: Tim Violet
  (507) 625-1882
  Smoking is banned in the workplace. The company sponsors smoking cessation.

- Salina-Kansas Journal
  Salina, Kan.
  Contact: Harris Rayl, editor
  (913) 823-6363
  Smoking is banned throughout the entire building.

- Westlake Community Hospital
  Melrose Park, Ill.
  Contact: Leonard Muller, president
  (312) 681-3000
  Under a new policy, only nonsmokers are hired. Starting July 1, 1985, smoking was permitted in only one section of the cafeteria. Patients may smoke only with the permission of their physician.

FLORIDA/GEORGIA/ALABAMA/LOUISIANA/ NORTH CAROLINA/TEXAS/OKLAHOMA

- Muse Air Lines
  Dallas Tex.
  Contact: Scott Hamilton, director of corporate affairs
  (214) 352-2828
  There is no smoking in the office areas; smoking is restricted to designated areas only. All Muse airplanes are totally smokefree.

- City Federal Savings and Loan Association
  Birmingham, Ala.
  Contact: Elizabeth Mengel
  (205) 320-6000
  The company pays $20 per month to all employees who abstain from smoking at both the workplace and home.

- Pratt and Whitney Aircraft
  West Palm Beach, Fla.
  Contact: Keith Klischer
  (305) 840-3076
  There are separate work areas for smokers and nonsmokers, air cleaners and fans are available at no charge to employees, and smoking cessation classes are offered on a regular basis.

Appendix B: Eight Steps to
Establish a Nonsmoking Policy

The Smoking Policy Institute (Seattle, Washington) suggested an eight-step program to organizations interested in establishing a nonsmoking policy:[1]

R REVIEW THE RESEARCH

The first step to successful nonsmoking policy implementation is a comprehensive understanding of the rationale behind the introduction of smoking restrictions and a review of the many possible alternatives.

E EMPLOYEE INVOLVEMENT

Stringent smoking restrictions will present a hardship to certain employees based on their addiction to nicotine. Participatory management, which involves employees in policy development and implementation, is the key to success.

S STRATEGIC PLAN

Resolution of any problem in a corporate environment requires the development of a strategy—clean indoor air policies are no exception.

T TIME FOR TRANSITION

As with any change, people need time to make the required adjustments. Organizations need different timetables for policy implementation based on differences in employee populations.

R REDUCE EXPOSURE TO SMOKE

It is possible to get so involved with policy development that an organization loses sight of the goal of the policy—a smokefree workplace.

I INCENTIVES FOR EMPLOYEES

Many employees use the reduced opportunities to smoke at work as an incentive to quit smoking. Assisting in these efforts is a wise corporate investment.

C CLEAR COMMUNICATIONS

A lot of time, energy, and resources go into the Tobacco Industry's efforts to keep people smoking. Any countereducation effort needs to be sophisticated in its message and delivery.

T TAKE A BOW

Organizations that have successfully implemented stringent smoking policies tend to attract very favorable media attention.

NOTE

1. William L. Weis, *Toward a Smoke-free Work Environment* (Seattle: Fresh Air for Non-Smokers, n.d.). See also Leah L. Woodruff, "Life Insurer Plans for a Smoke-free Office," *Business and Health* (November 1984): 22-23; U.S. Public Health Service, *No Smoking: A Decision Maker's Guide to Reducing Smoking at the Worksite* (Washington, D.C.: Washington Business Group on Health, 1985); and American Lung Association, *Taking Executive Action: Freedom from Smoking at Work* (1985).

9

CONCLUSIONS AND SUMMARY

Employers who choose to implement nonsmoking policies have everything to gain and little to lose, if. . . . The "if" involves attention to the "how" of implementation. Any program that is installed in the workplace demands attention to assessing needs, defining the problem(s), analyzing the problem(s), generating alternative solutions, selecting the "best" strategy, implementing the strategy effectively, and constantly evaluating and revising as time passes. To follow up on a new program employers must *monitor and control*. Let us define these two terms as:

Monitoring: Accumulation of data on operations.

Control: The use of data accumulated to correct or change the system.

Clearly, every company or agency that restricts or bans smoking will gather data on operations—expressions of employee attitudes, grievances filed, evidences of policy violation, problems with air recirculation, and others. All managers must ultimately use the accumulated data to correct or change the system (Chapters 6 and 7 showed how many firms went from "smoking only in designated offices and rooms" to outright bans because of problems of uniform enforcement, ventilation, and so forth).

The authors suggest five objectives for any monitoring and control system:

1. Resource utilization
2. Program accomplishment

3. Security

4. Quality

5. Human development

All of these are obvious as they apply to no smoking in the workplace. Yet the fifth is most often ignored. Yes, management is clearly interested in how well resources are utilized. Yes, we must and can properly insist upon accomplishing the program we are monitoring. Security is obvious (not just fire safety, but the healthy compliance of workers with a policy—everything from sneaking smokes in closets and restrooms to measurements of morale). Quality is today's watchword for companies and government agencies. In a competitive market any edge on quality can be a determining factor of success (recall the stories of hospitals who went nonsmoking and quickly learned that it paid off). But too often we forget to use the data accumulated in our control systems to *develop our human resources*. There are many ways this can be done in implementing a nonsmoking policy in the workplace—consulting with workers from the beginning; securing their ideas, needs, and input; letting them help design the nonsmoking policy; involving them in the implementation of the program and subsequent evaluation and appraisal of its success or failure; and so many other ways, all of which develop our human resources and maximize our return on investment in our most valuable resource—people.

Whatever control system an organization uses to track its nonsmoking program (attitude surveys, suggestion boxes, employee newsletters, open meetings with the CEO, whatever), all effective control systems have the following characteristics:

1. They are designed to deal with and reflect the specific activity.

2. They report deviations promptly.

3. They are forward looking.

4. They point out exceptions at critical points.

5. They are objective.

6. They are flexible.

7. They reflect the organizational pattern.

8. They are economical.

9. They are understandable.

10. They lead to corrective action.

Each of these ten characteristics deserves a chapter of its own, in one sense. For instance, characteristic 6. The authors have called for uniformity of enforcement. One of the authors has been a labor arbitrator for nearly twenty years, and uniformity of enforcement is often seen as the *sine qua non* of arbitral rulings on discipline and discharge. Still, as with any control system, supervisors and managers must remember they are dealing with human beings, flesh and blood people, people with feelings and needs. Flexibility, especially during the initial stages of installing a total ban, may be the key to success.

Certain managerial and supervisory behaviors will help whenever implementing any policy that may be controversial with 20 percent or so of any organization's employees. To maximize the likelihood of developing controls with these characteristics, the manager should:

1. Maintain an "adult" view of controls
2. Encourage subordinates' participation in setting standards
3. Introduce flexibility in the control system
4. Be sensitive to personal needs and social pressures in administering controls

These behaviors are especially true of managers involved with nonsmoking policies and progams. The responses should not be "parental"—that is, "We warned you, now we're going to punish you!" "Gotcha!" or, "You are in trouble now, wait'll human resources finds out about this!" Responses should not be "childish"—tantrums, name calling, affixing blame, and so forth. Rather, an "adult" manager asks, What happened? What should be done about it? How can I help? Readers can surely recall their own war stories of different types of managerial behavior. If smoking is as addictive as claimed, managers must be prepared for the long haul. "Smoking reform is no sport for the short winded." If the manager does not take this approach, subordinates are more likely to:

1. Fail to accept objectives as legitimate
2. Feel the standards of performance are too high
3. Believe that measurements are inappropriate
4. Fear negative feedback
5. Perceive the source of control as "illegitimate"
6. Play games with the controls
7. Engage in sabotage or negative behaviors

The authors heard a number of war stories during their research and writing of this book that suggest the lengths some workers will go to when managers "misbehave." We hope some of these accounts were only apocryphal. One, for instance, involved a blue collar worker caught smoking in a restroom by a top manager. The worker threatened to "get" the manager if the smoking incident were reported. The worker was ultimately fired for violating corporate policy, and the manager lived for months afterwards in fear of some kind of reprisal or other "negative behavior." (It turned out this firm did not hire smokers at all, but made no serious effort at reference verification before or immediately after employment.)

During the course of this book we have looked at the scope of the non-smoking controversy—the acrimony, the debates, the rebuttals from all sides, and the emerging trends and directions. We have also addressed the costs of smoking—lost lives, sickness, loss of worker productivity, the costs of passive or secondhand smoking, the wide range of less obvious costs to the employer of smoking in the workplace (damage to furniture, cleaning costs, insurance premiums, and so on). We have considered the public health issues and the changes in societal attitudes toward smoking. The long-range impact of all of these value shifts seems to be a decline in the numbers or percentages of smokers (still, smokers are using more cigarettes, but fewer people smoke). Smoking cessation efforts will likely be more difficult with the remaining hard-core smokers. Some acrimony has now entered the debate, battle lines are forming, voices are more strident. Management must be careful to play a moderating, even a mediative, role in implementing and enforcing a nonsmoking policy. It is worth the effort, perfectly legal, but takes careful planning and sincere efforts to assure worker participation.

Several chapters reviewed various case studies of nonsmoking efforts around the country. A very few employers won't hire smokers at all. A majority have nonsmoking policies (at least in the private sector). The trends seem to be toward outright bans on smoking in the workplace. If management will properly monitor and control its nonsmoking program, once a policy is crafted and implemented, if management will remember all the objectives of a monitoring and control system, if management will seek to design effective control systems, if managers will act properly so workers will respond properly, then such nonsmoking programs will clearly succeed.

What is the definition of success? Healthier workers, a more productive work force, a more competitive organization in the marketplace, cleaner air for all of us, a cleaner work site, cost-containment in health care, and a society that benefits from healthier citizens who live longer lives. That is basically what this book has been all about.

SELECTED BIBLIOGRAPHY

BOOKS

American Cancer Society. *The Dangers of Smoking, the Benefits of Quitting*. New York: 1982.

Califano, Joseph A. Jr. *Governing America*. New York: Simon and Schuster, 1981.

Diehl, Harold S. *Tobacco and Your Health: The Smoking Controversy*. New York: McGraw-Hill, 1969.

Fritschler, A. Lee. *Smoking and Politics*. Englewood Cliffs, N.J.: Prentice-Hall, 1969.

Morgan, Hal. *Symbols of America*. New York: Viking Penguin, 1986.

National Institute of Drug Abuse. *Research on Smoking Behavior*. Washington, D.C.: U.S. Government Printing Office, 1977.

National Research Council. *Environmental Tobacco Smoke: Measuring Exposures and Assessing Health Effects*. Washington, D.C.: National Academy Press, 1986.

Skinner, Wiliam Iverson. *Tobacco and Health: The Other Side of the Coin*. New York: Vantage Press, 1970.

Sobel, Robert. *They Satisfy*. Garden City, N.Y.: Doubleday, 1978.

Tollison, Robert D. *Smoking and Society: Toward a More Balanced Assessment*. Lexington, Mass.: Lexington Books, 1986.

Troyer, Ronald J. and Markle, Gerald E. *Cigarettes: The Battle Over Smoking*. New Brunswick, N.J.: Rutgers University Press, 1983.

Whelan, Elizabeth M. *A Smoking Gun: How the Tobacco Industry Gets Away with Murder*. Philadelphia: George F. Stickley Co., 1984.

Winter, Ruth. *The Scientific Case Against Smoking*. New York: Crown Publishers, 1980.

ARTICLES AND RELATED PUBLICATIONS

Bock, Fred G. "Nonsmokers and Cigarette Smoke: A Modified Perception of Risk." *Science* 215 (1982): 197.

Buckley, William F., Jr. "The Weed." In *The Tobacco Industry in Transition*, ed. William R. Finger. Lexington, Mass.: Lexington Books, 1981.

Cameron Charles. "Lung Cancer and Smoking." *Atlantic* 197 (1) (1956): 71-75.

Cascio, Wayne F. "Costing the Effects of Smoking at the Work Place." In *Costing Human Resources: The Financial Impact of Behavior in Organizations*. Boston: PWS-Kent Publishing Co., 1987: 80-97.

Fielding, Jonathan E. "Smoking: Health Effects and Control." *The New England Journal of Medicine* 313 (9) (1985): 555-61.

Foote, Emerson. "Advertising and Tobacco." *Journal of the American Medical Association* 245 (16) (1981): 1667-68.

Garfinkel, Lawrence. "The Impact of Low Tar/Nicotine Cigarettes." *World Smoking and Health* 5 (2): 4-8.

Hymowitz, Norman. "Personalizing the Risk of Cigarette Smoking." *Journal of the Medical Society of New Jersey* 77 (1980): 579-82.

Lilienfeld, Abraham M. "The Case Against the Cigarette." *The Nation* 194 (13) (1962): 277-80.

Little, Clarence Cook. "The Public and Smoking: Fear or Calm Deliberation." *The Atlantic* 200 (6) (1957): 74-76.

Timmins, William M. "Smoking versus Nonsmoking at Work: A Survey of Public Agency Policy and Practice." *Public Personnel Management*, 16 (3) (1987): 221-34.

INDEX

About the Authors

DR. WILLIAM M. TIMMINS was Professor of Personnel Administration and Labor/Management Relations in the Graduate School of Management, Brigham Young University (Provo, Utah) from 1974. He was Adjunct Professor of Political Science at the University of Utah (Salt Lake City) for over ten years and also taught at several other colleges and universities. He died in February of 1989.

CLARK BRIGHTON TIMMINS, a graduate of the University of Utah in English in 1988, is currently completing an MFA. He has lived in Guatemala and traveled extensively throughout Europe and the United States. He currently works part-time as a computer center supervisor. He is a published poet and writer.